Circle Time Sing-Alongs & Fingerplays

**Written by Susan Finkel
and Karen Seberg**

Illustrated by Gary Mohrman

Teaching & Learning Company

1204 Buchanan St., P.O. Box 10
Carthage, IL 62321

This book belongs to

_____

The activity portrayed on the front cover is described on page 20.

Cover by Gary Mohrman

Copyright © 1996, Teaching & Learning Company

ISBN No. 1-57310-066-8

Printing No. 987654321

Teaching & Learning Company
1204 Buchanan St., P.O. Box 10
Carthage, IL 62321

Table of Contents

Table of Themes

Every reasonable attempt has been made to identify copyrighted material.

Dear Teacher or Parent,

How often have you said these words *OK, everyone, time for circle time. Let's gather on the rug!* and then thought to yourself "What should we do today?" This book will help you through those times when you are tired of the same old ideas. We've taken many familiar children's songs and created some great circle time activities for you to try. In addition, we'll give you ideas for originating your own songs, using these familiar tunes.

What is circle time?
Circle times are large or small group gatherings. During your circle time, you may present daily or weekly themes or concepts. You may use books, pictures, flannel boards, concrete materials, share experiences and sing songs!

What is the best way to do circle time?
There is no "best" way. Each teacher has his or her own style. You can gather ideas for your circle times by reading books, attending classes and observing other teachers. Eventually, you will develop your own style, what works best for you and your class. Be aware that you may need to adjust your style from year to year, or even as the school year progresses, depending on the changes in your children.

Some circle time hints:
Establish a set place in your classroom to gather. It should be out of the room's main traffic pattern. A round or oval rug makes a great visual cue for the children as they come together. If possible, locate your circle time space near a window.

Have an easel, chalkboard or flannel board nearby for using visual aids or recording the children's ideas.

If you prefer a "backup" when you sing, use a tape, CD or record player. You don't need to be a great singer to have great circle times, but you will need to know how to use this equipment.

Plan your circle times for the same time each day. Children need a consistent schedule for each day's activities; they feel security in knowing the sequence of a day's planned events. Create a consistent pattern of activities within your circle time as well.

Name your circle time whatever you wish: morning meeting, group time, together time or something else unique to your children.

Use concrete items whenever possible.

If you find the children are not responding to a particular activity or song, STOP. Try again later, on another day or in another way.

Sincerely,

Susan   Karen

Susan Finkel and Karen Seberg

About This Book

Circle times are an important part of the early learner's day. The attachment young children develop to routine is supported with daily or regular circle time experiences. The socialization with daily or regular circle time settings are important acquistions. The value of shared group experiences is evident in the opportunities presented to each child to contribute as an individual and participate as a member of a team. Plus circle times are great occasions to relax, learn, have some fun and–SING!

The circle times in this book use familiar children's songs as a starting point for many theme-related activities. (You may find the songs have regional variations.) Songs are arranged alphabetically and you will also find a list of cross-referenced themes. Included for each song are its words and some of the following activities or suggestions: visuals, manipulatives and concrete objectives; actions and movements; variations; art and sensory activities; discussion ideas; changes in the classroom environment; sources of recorded versions.

Following are the symbols used throughout the book to identify the different themes.

Animals

Letter Recognition

Body Awareness

Make Your Own Music

Classroom Friends

Making Comparisons

Community

Nutrition

Families

Spatial Concepts

Feelings

Transportation

There is a section called "Books to Share" where you will find books on the themes to use with your children. We've included simple patterns for you to try. Go ahead! Try and feel free to create new words for all of the songs you know!

Aiken Drum

There was a man lived in the moon, in the moon, in the moon,
There was a man lived in the moon,
And his name was Aiken Drum.
(chorus)
And he played upon his ladle, his ladle, his ladle,
He played upon his ladle,
And his name was Aiken Drum.
(verses)
His head was made of cheese, cheese, cheese . . .
His eyes were made of meatballs . . .
His hair was made of spaghetti . . .

Families

Circle Time Starter
Sing the song with the group. Say, "Aiken Drum is a silly name for a man who lives in the moon. Why do you think his mom and dad named him Aiken Drum?"

Props/Visual Aids
Bring a book to class listing baby names and their origins. Look up and read the children's names and meanings and list them on a large group chart.

Talk About
Send a note home to parents (see page 9) asking them to provide information about their child's name. Have children share their notes with the class.

To Extend This Circle Time
Have children choose new and/or silly names for themselves. Make a record of everyone's new name and why he or she thinks it would be a good name to have. Provide name tags for the children to wear and call them by their new names for the day. (Be sure to inform parents of this day's plans.)

Feelings

Circle Time Starter
Vary the words to the song to show Aiken Drum expressing different feelings and emotions. You might sing, "His mouth was always smiling, smiling, smiling" or "His eyes were very sad, sad, sad."

Props/Visual Aid
Reproduce the patterns on page 10. Color, laminate and use pieces of rolled masking tape to help the face pieces adhere to the flannel board. With a piece of yarn, make a large circle on the flannel board for Aiken Drum's face. As you sing the new words to the song, place the face pieces on the flannel board to illustrate different emotions.

Talk About

Have the children change the expressions on their faces as you sing about Aiken Drum's feelings. Change the expression on your face and ask the children if they can tell how you are feeling. Ask, "Why do you think Aiken Drum felt happy? Tired? Sad?" Write a story about Aiken Drum on chart paper using the children's responses.

To Extend This Circle Time

You will need washable face paints or crayons and paint shirts to protect clothing. Divide the children into pairs and have them take turns painting their partners' faces. Can they make a sad face, happy face or tired face? Before you begin, be aware of any children with allergies or sensitive skin.

nutrition

Circle Time Starter

Aiken Drum is a man made of food; each part of his body will be a different type. The children will love choosing the words to the song using their favorite foods.

Props/Visual Aids

As you write the song together, draw a simple picture of Aiken Drum on chart paper to remind the children of the choices made for each body part.

Talk About

Aiken Drum can be composed of healthy foods; junk foods; breakfast, lunch or dinner foods. Talk about the basic food groups and the USDA's "Food Guide Pyramid" choosing foods from each group:

fats, oils and sweets	milk, yogurt and cheese
vegetables	meat, poultry, fish, beans, eggs and nuts
fruit	bread, rice, pasta and cereals

To Extend This Circle Time

Provide the art center with magazines, safety scissors and glue, or supply the children with food pictures you have already cut out. Give each child a large sheet of paper to make his or her own Aiken Drum.

Tapes and CDs

Carfra, Pat. "Aiken Drum" from *Songs for Sleepyheads and Out-of-Beds.* Lullaby Lady Productions, 1984.

Lehman, Peg. "Aiken Drum" from *Critters in the Choir.* Pal Music, 1989.

McGrath, Bob. "Aikendrum" from *Sing Along with Bob, Vol. 1.* Kids' Records, 1984.

Raffi. "Aikendrum" from *The Singable Songs Collection.* Shoreline/A&M Records, 1988.

Dear Parents,

We will be talking about our names this week. Please return this form by

_____.

Thanks!

My name is _____.
My parents named me that because

_____.

If I could choose a new name, It would be

_____.

The Alphabet Song

A, B, C, D, E, F, G,
H, I, J, K, L, M, N, O, P,
Q, R, S,
T, U, V,
W, X, Y and Z
Now I know my ABCs,
Next time won't you sing with me?

Letter Recognition

Aa
Bb Cc

Circle Time Starter

Use this song to facilitate letter recognition. Display all the letters of the alphabet on your flannel board or other accessible area. Sing the song and stop suddenly at different letters. "A, B, C, D, E, F, G, H, I, J, K, who can find the letter *K*?" or "A, B, C, D, E, F, G, H, I, J, K, L, M, N, O, P, Q, R, S, whose name has an *S* in it?"

Props/Visual Aids

Decorate an empty, plastic five-gallon ice cream bucket. Cut a 4" (10 cm) hole in the lid, large enough for a hand to pass through easily. Place the letters of the alphabet inside the bucket, either felt cut-outs or plastic magnetic letters. Allow the children to take turns drawing out letters as you sing the song, stopping at the chosen letter. Display the selected letters on your flannel board or magnetic board.

Talk About

Find objects in the classroom that start with the selected letter and list them. Ask parents to help in adding to the list from objects at home. The children will be excited to see how long they can make the list for a particular letter.

To Extend This Circle Time

Have the children draw out letters and place on the board in random order. Invite them to sing the alphabet song in the new "mixed-up" way, "Q, T, S, M, I, K, B . . . "

Circle Time Starter

There are several children's songs that use this well-known melody. "Twinkle, Twinkle, Little Star"; "Baa, Baa, Black Sheep" and "Little Arabella Miller" are all sung to this tune. Because of its familiarity, this melody is a great base for creating your own song. Begin by reading a story to the group on your selected theme or by webbing or listing the concepts the class already knows about the theme.

Props/Visual Aids

Use a chart pad and markers to write the group's ideas and then the words to the song. It is important for the children to see the words they are creating.

Talk About

Ask the group if they would like to write a song about the theme. You might say, "Let's write a song about all the things we know about fire safety. What should we say in our song?" Record their ideas on the chart pad. Explain that "we usually sing ABC to this tune, but today we will sing our new words." You can be flexible with rhyming and rhythms, but be sure to keep the final version so the class can sing it over and over.

To Extend This Circle Time

Send copies of the words home with the children so they can share the song with their families. If you create songs for several units, compile them to make a class songbook. Include some blank pages to allow the children to add their own illustrations. Each child will have a collection of songs to take home at the end of the year.

Tapes and CDs

Greg and Steve. "ABC Rock" from *We All Live Together, Vol. 1*. Youngheart Records, 1975.

Koch, Fred. "A, B, C" from *This Lil' Cow*. Red Rover Records, 1983.

McGrath, Bob. "A, B, C, D" from *Sing Along with Bob, Vol. 1*. Kids' Records, 1984.

Monet, Lisa. "ABC Song" from *Circle Time: Songs and Rhymes for the Very Young*. Monet Productions, 1986.

Baby Bumblebee

I'm bringing home a baby bumblebee,
Won't my mama be so proud of me,
I'm bringing home a baby bumblebee,
Bzzz, Bzzz, Bzzz, Bzzz, Bzzz.

Animals

Circle Time Starter

Vary the words to the song by using a variety of animals and the sounds they make. You might also want to change the mama's reaction depending on the type of animal.

"I'm bringing home baby chimpanzee,
Won't my mama be so glad to see . . ."
"I'm bringing home a baby rattlesnake,
Won't my mama shiver and shake . . ."
"I'm bringing home a baby elephant,
Unless my mama says that I can't . . ."
"I'm bringing home a baby dinosaur,
Won't my mama let out a big roar . . ."

Props/Visual Aids

Cut out pictures of baby animals to hold as you sing the song. Use the patterns on pages 16 and 17, and have the children color them. Share several of the wonderful picture books of baby animals (see "Books to Share" on page 92) available from your library. Invite the children to bring plush baby animals from home.

Talk About

Ask if any of the children have or had baby animals in their homes. "How did you take care of it? Did it need special care because it was a baby? How fast did it grow up?"

To Extend This Circle Time

Invite the children to bring in their own baby pictures. Take photographs of the children and display the current and baby pictures together on a poster. Talk about how the children have changed since they were babies. Don't forget to add your own pictures to the display!

Families

Circle Time Starter

Vary the words to the song by using names of other members of the family. You might sing, "I'm bringing home a grandma bumblebee."

Props/Visual Aids

Use the patterns on page 18 to create flannel board pieces. As you sing the song, change the characteristics of the generic bee to match those in the verse.

Talk About

People in different families use different names for their family members: Mom, Mama, Mommy, Mother. Ask, "What word do you use for *mother* in your family? What word do you use for *father*?" Discuss multicultural words and the words used for family members in different languages. Here are a few examples:

	Mother	Father	Sister	Brother	Grandma	Grandpa
Chinese:	mu ch'in	fu ch'in	chieh mei	hsiung ti	tsu mu	tsu fu
Japanese:	haha	chichi	shimai	kydai	sobo	sofu
German:	die mutter	der vater	die schwester	der bruder	die grobmama	der grobvater
French:	mère	père	soeur	frère	grand-mère	grand-père
Spanish:	madre	padre	hermana	hermano	abuelita	abuelito

To Extend This Circle Time

Create a bee family tree. Supply the children with black and yellow construction paper, glue, markers and safety scissors. Use the patterns on page 18 for the bee's body. The children can cut strips of black paper to glue on for stripes and draw other features with washable markers or crayons. As they make their own bees, talk about what member of the family each child's bee is. Do their bees have names? Use large poster board to display the bees, starting at the top with grandma and grandpa bees and drawing connecting lines between generations with the baby bees at the bottom of the poster.

Circle Time Starter

Sing this song when the class is learning the letter *B*. You can vary the words to the song when working with other letters. "I'm bringing home five fireflies for Fred" or "I'm bringing home a little lunch for Lee."

Props/Visual Aids

Bring or find in the classroom a number of items that begin with the specified letter. You will also need chart paper and markers.

Talk About

Have the children suggest words that start with the letter *B*. You can use the collected items as prompts. Record the children's words on chart paper and create new verses for the song using their words. You might sing, "I'm bringing home a big blue ball for Bruce."

To Extend This Circle Time

Make *B* bags. You will need lunch-size paper bags, glue and pictures cut from magazines, or reproduce the pictures on page 19. Have the children glue pictures of things starting with the letter *B* on their bags. Ask the children to take their bags with them and find things at home that start with the letter *B*. Invite them to bring the *B* items to school in the bag to share with the class.

Tapes and CDs

Beall, Pamela Conn, and Susan Hagen Nipp. "Baby Bumblebee" from *Wee Sing Silly Songs*. Price Stern Sloan, 1986.

Tia. "Baby Bumblebee (Baby Dinosaur)" from *Tia's Dino-Stew Zoo*. Tia's Quacker Tunes, 1987.

Various Performers. "Baby Bumblebee" from *Disney's Silly Songs*. Walt Disney Records, 1988.

16

The Bear Went over the Mountain

The bear went over the mountain,
The bear went over the mountain,
The bear went over the mountain,
To see what he could see.

And all that he could see,
And all that he could see,
Was the other side of the mountain,
The other side of the mountain,
The other side of the mountain,
Was all that he could see.

Circle Time Starter

Vary the words to this song by substituting other animal names. If your group is learning about farm animals, sing about the cow, pig or horse who went over the mountain. For zoo animals, sing about the zebra, lion or monkey.

Props/Visual Aids

Let each child in the group choose a different plush or plastic animal to hold up as you sing the song. You may also use pictures of the animals to place on a flannel board. Provide the children with animal masks to wear as they sing the song. Use the patterns on pages 24 to 26. They may walk around the classroom pretending to be cows, lions or bears going over the mountain.

Talk About

Write a group story about the animals going over the mountain. Using a large sheet of paper, record the children's ideas. Ask, "Why would the cow want to go over the mountain?" "What does the cow see at the top of the mountain?" "What might the farmer say when she finds out the cow is on top of the mountain?"

To Extend This Circle Time

Place masks of animals in the dramatic play corner of your classroom. Encourage children to build mountains out of wooden blocks. Provide small plastic animals to "climb" over the block mountains.

Circle Time Starter

Vary the words to this song by using the names of children in the group. You can use it as a morning greeting song, a way to check attendance or as a way to help everyone learn the names of class-mates.

> "Sally came to school today,
> Sally came to school today,
> Sally came to school today,
> Whom did she see?
>
> She saw Kevin,
> She saw Kevin,
> She saw Kevin,
> Kevin is at school."

Props/Visual Aids

Use a pair of binoculars or a large magnifying glass to identify a child for the next verse or spy through a cardboard tube "periscope" to see each child.

Talk About

You can use this song to get your group going every morning. It is important to follow a routine for your circle times. Children need to know that after the song, it is time for calendar or weather or to hear about free play choices. Children also need to become familiar with others in the class, especially when there are new children coming into a group. Use this song as a way to learn everyone's names. Children can choose the next child to be included in the verse: "Whom do you see, Sally?" "I see Kevin!"

To Extend This Circle Time

Take pictures of the children in your group or ask parents to bring photographs from home. Use these in a bulletin board display or as flash cards to identify the children in the group.

Community

Circle Time Starter
Vary the words to this song by naming people's occupations in the neighborhood or community along with the job or service they perform. Sing, "The nurse will keep you healthy," "The firefighter puts out the fires" or "The baker makes the doughnuts." You could also sing, "The bear went to the grocery store" or other familiar places in your community.

Props/Visual Aids
Use pictures, hats or other real items as you sing this song.

Talk About
Talk about the people in the community. Use the group's ideas to write the song.

To Extend This Circle Time
Plan a field trip to visit some of the people in your community. Parents can be a great resource! Invite them to come to your classroom to talk about their jobs. Provide props from different community/neighborhood people in your dramatic play area.

22

Circle Time Starter

Vary the words to this song by having the bear go under, through or around the mountain.

Visual Aids/Props

Give each child a bear-shaped plastic counter and an arch-shaped wooden block. The children can move their bears along as they sing the new words to the song. On a flannel board, place a picture of a mountain and a bear. The children may manipulate the pieces to match the verse of the song.

Talk About

Make a group list of things the children climb over, under, through or between. Using magazine pictures, make a group collage of these concepts.

To Extend This Circle Time

Use a small table, large blocks or wooden climbing stairs to provide large motor experiences for the children. Rearrange the classroom or playground equipment into an obstacle course for the children to climb over, under or through. Have the children make paper bag bear puppets using the patterns on page 26.

Tapes and CDs

Beall, Pamela Conn, and Susan Hagen Nipp. "The Bear Went over the Mountain" from *Wee Sing Silly Songs.* Price Stern Sloan, 1986.

McGrath, Bob. "The Bear Went over the Mountain" from *Sing Along with Bob, Vol. 1.* Kids' Records, 1984.

Roth, Kevin. "The Bear Went over the Mountain" from *Oscar, Bingo and Buddies.* CMS Records, 1986.

25

26

Do Your Ears Hang Low?

Sung to the tune of "Turkey in the Straw"

Do your ears hang low?
Do they wobble to and fro?
Can you tie them in a knot,
Can you tie them in a bow?
Can you throw them over your shoulder
Like a continental soldier?
Do your ears hang low?

Do your ears hang high?
Do they reach up to the sky?
Are they curly when they're wet,
Are they shaggy when they're dry?
Can you toss them over your shoulder
Like a continental soldier?
Do your ears hang high?

Body Awareness

Circle Time Starter

As you sing the song, invite the children to make up actions for the words. Ask, "How would you show tying a knot?" "How would you show curly ears?"

Props/Visual Aids

Purchase a large pair of ears at a costume or novelty store or use the patterns on page 30. Wear the ears as you sing the song. Allow each child to have an opportunity to try on the ears. You may want to have a hand mirror available. The children will enjoy seeing their altered reflections!

Talk About

Ask, "Can ears really be tied in a bow? Can you throw them over your shoulder? What if you could?" Write a group story about the possibilities and invite the children to illustrate it.

To Extend This Circle Time

Provide magazines and safety scissors at the art center. Ask the children to find and cut out pictures of ears. Glue them on a large piece of tagboard to make an ear collage. Start a collection of clip-on earrings. Include them with your other props and clothing in the dramatic play area.

Families

Circle Time Starter

Members of a family often resemble each other physically. Children may share eye color with parents or grandparents, have freckles in the same places or ears that look the same. Children might have the same sense of humor, walk or throw a ball just like another family member. As you do these activities, be sensitive that some children in your class may not live with their birth families.

Props/Visual Aids

Ask the children to bring pictures of the people in their families, including moms, dads, grandparents and siblings. Label the pictures so they may be returned easily. Don't forget to bring photographs of your own family!

Talk About

In small groups of three or four children, share the pictures of each family. Discuss similarities and differences. "Look, Cassie looks like her mom. They have the same hair color. But her brother looks like her dad."

To Extend This Circle Time

Make copies of the note to the parents on page 31 and send one home with each child.

Circle Time Starter

As you sing the song, ask the children to listen for the words with opposite meanings. Some of their responses will include: low/high, (wobble) to/fro, knot/bow, throw/toss, curly/shaggy, wet/dry.

Props/Visual Aids

Gather materials to demonstrate the opposites in the song. Some props might include ropes for tying, beanbags for tossing, sponges for wet and dry. Divide the children into groups of two and assign each a pair of words. Sing the song, allowing plenty of time for the children to act out the opposite words they have been given.

Talk About

Make a list of other comparisons. Ask, "What is the opposite of *tall?* The opposite of *loud?* The opposite of *fast?*" Encourage the children to find examples of opposites in the classroom. Ask them to continue looking for opposites at home and set aside time to share their findings.

To Extend This Circle Time

Set up a sink float activity in your science area. Fill a plastic wash tub or dishpan with about 3" (8 cm) of water. On a tray, place a variety of items which will sink or float. Allow the children time to experiment, and be sure to keep towels close at hand for quick cleanups!

Tapes and CDs

Beall, Pamela Conn, and Susan Hagen Nipp. "Do Your Ears Hang Low?" from *Wee Sing Silly Songs*. Price Stern Sloan, 1989.

McGrath, Bob. "Do Your Ears Hang Low?" from *Sing Along with Bob, Vol. 2*. Kids' Records, 1985.

Sharon, Lois and Bram. "Do Your Ears Hang Low?" from *Stay Tuned*. Elephant Records, 1987.

Various Performers. "Do Your Ears Hang Low?" from *Disney's Children's Favorites, Vol. 4*. Walt Disney Records, 1990.

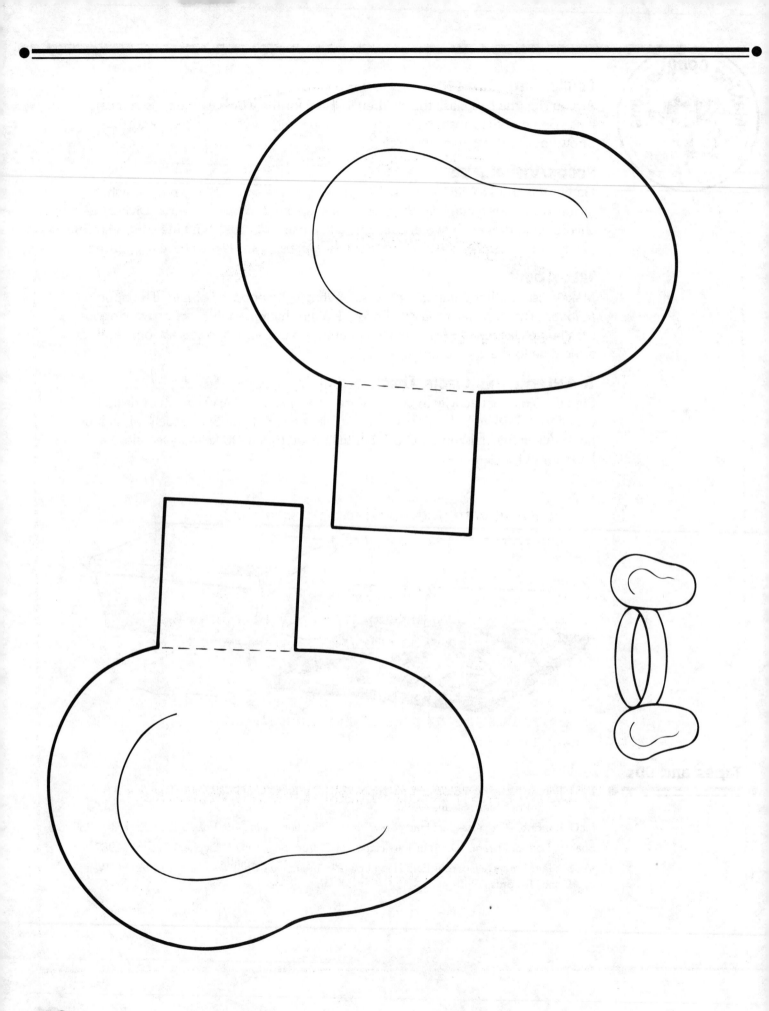

Dear Parents,

We are discussing family resemblances!

Thank you for sending pictures of your family to our class.

Please sit with your child tonight and share pictures of yourself as a child.

Tell a story about when you were your child's age. If you have photographs of your parents and grandparents as children, talk about those as well.

Enjoy this special time of sharing with your child!

The Eency Weency Spider

The eency weency spider went up the water spout.
Down came the rain and washed the spider out.
Out came the sun and dried up all the rain,
And the eency weency spider went up the spout again.

Animals

Circle Time Starter

Use this song's simple melody for your own words. Children will enjoy helping create silly lyrics about animals. Two examples:

The big, spotted cow walked down the farmer's path.
"Moo," said the cow, "I'm going to take a bath!"
Out came the farmer to dry off the cow's back,
Then the cow and the farmer lay down to take a nap.

The soft, brown puppy chewed on a bone.
"Woof," said the puppy, "I think I'm all alone."
The puppy went looking for another friend,
He found his sister, now the song can end.

Props/Visual Aids

Use a piece of chart paper to write the new words for the song. Say, "I think we should write our own song today! What animal should we choose?" Use as many of the children's suggestions as possible.

Talk About

This song sounds best if the phrases end with rhyming words. Discuss words that sound alike and words that do not end the same. The phrases do not have to rhyme exactly but can serve as an introduction to rhyming sounds. Your children will love writing their own songs and will request their versions over and over. To help you remember the words, write them on an index card.

To Extend This Circle Time

After sharing other books that use a song as the story (Raffi has a series of books entitled Songs to Read), have the class illustrate their song. Compile the pictures in a class book to read and sing again and again.

Circle Time Starter

Vary the words to the song to ascribe feelings or emotions to the spider. Ask, "What if the spider was very tired? What if the spider was grumpy? Happy? What kind of voice would you use to sing the song?"

Props/Visual Aids

Reproduce the spider patterns on page 35. Laminate and use pieces of rolled masking tape to help them adhere to the flannel board. Cut pictures of faces showing different emotions from magazines. Prepare these for use on the flannel board.

Talk About

Sing the song, describing different emotions of the spider. Place the spiders and the faces you have cut out on the flannel board. Ask, "Which spider are we singing about now? Which face looks like the spider's feelings? Can you look like you feel that way, too?"

To Extend This Circle Time

Make spider headbands. Each child will need eight strips of black paper, approximately 1" x 11" (2.5 x 28 cm). Demonstrate how to accordion fold the strips. Glue the folded strips to a 2" (5 cm) wide strip of black paper, long enough to fit around a child's head. Children may decorate the headbands with glitter, stickers or paint. Invite the children to wear their headbands as they act out variations of the song.

Circle Time Starter

Sing the song using these variations:

Size: The great big spider

Speed: The very slow spider, the very tiny spider, the very fast spider

Silly: The very mixed up spider (combine several of the above)

Spatial: Have the spider crawl over, under, in, beneath the water spout.

Props/Visual Aids

Find pictures of different types of spiders and display them on the bulletin board. Ask the class to help you label them as fast, slow, big, tiny and so on. You can also use the spider illustrations on page 35 to create your own cue cards for the song. Color, cut out and laminate the cards or cover with clear adhesive paper to make them more durable.

Talk About

Create actions for your new verses. Ask, "How would a very slow spider crawl?" Encourage acting with the child's whole body and showing a variety of facial expressions.

Sing the song with the voice of the very tiny spider and again like the very fast spider. Ask, "What might happen if the great big spider tries to crawl up a water spout?"

To Extend This Circle Time

Create a spiderweb in your classroom. Using yarn, wrap and weave strands around doorknobs, table legs and shelves in a small area of your room. You could also make a web on the playground equipment outside. Invite the class to move carefully through the web.

Tapes and CDs

Beall, Pamela Conn, and Susan Hagen Nipp. "The Eensy Weensy Spider" from *Wee Sing Children's Songs and Fingerplays*. Price Stern Sloan, 1990.

Little Richard. "Itsy Bitsy Spider" from *For Our Children*. Walt Disney Records, 1991.

Sharon, Lois and Bram. "The Eensy Weensy Spider" from *Great Big Hits*. A&M Records, Inc., 1992.

35

Going on a Lion Hunt

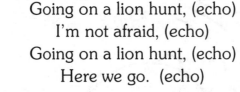

Going on a lion hunt, (echo)
I'm not afraid, (echo)
Going on a lion hunt, (echo)
Here we go. (echo)

Open the door, squeak, (echo)
Walk down the walk, (echo)
Open the gate, creak, (echo)
Walk down the road. (echo)

Choose a place to look and then add this refrain.
Can't go under it, (echo)
Can't go over it, (echo)
Have to go through it. (echo)

*When you finally find the lion, repeat all directions backwards
and very fast to get home safely.*

Circle Time Starter

Vary the words to hunt for any animal you choose. The group might hunt for tigers, bears, elephants or cows. When you find the animal at the end of the verse, ask the class for descriptive words to talk about it.

Props/Visual Aids

Use a chart pad and marker to sketch the story as you recite the words. Simple stick figures will work to give visual cues to the children; they will be especially helpful when reversing the order of the verses at the end of the chant.

Talk About

After you choose the animal you will be hunting, discuss the most likely places to look for that animal. "Where might a cow live? Where would we have to walk to get there?"

To Extend This Circle Time

Stage a lion (or other animal) hunt in your large muscle area. Decide what areas you will include and have the children help you create a trail with large blocks, chairs, tables and masking tape on the floor. Several children may choose to be the animals and will delight in roaring or otherwise scaring the rest of the "hunters" into hurrying home.

Circle Time Starter

Vary the words to the chant by using descriptions of your neighborhood. You might say, "Going to the bakery, want to get some cookies, walk past the fire station, cross the street, look both ways."

Props/Visual Aids

Gather items from the dramatic play area. Hats, plastic food, toy vehicles and animals can all be used with pantomime to provide visual hints to help the children remember the new words to the chant.

Talk About

Ask the children what stores or businesses are in the neighborhoods where they live. Ask, "How do you get to the store? What do you look for when you are there?" If there are no close businesses, children could describe how to get to a neighborhood friend's house and whom they will play with there.

To Extend This Circle Time

Arrange a field trip in the school's neighborhood. Talk about what the children will see and create a new chant before you go. Use the children's ideas and write the words down. When you return, you can recite the chant again and compare it to the actual experience.

Circle Time Starter

Vary the words to the chant using descriptive words, phrases or concepts relating to your unit theme. If your theme was fire safety, you might say, "Learning about fire safety, here are the rules, stop, drop and roll, crawl low in smoke, firefighters are our friends."

Props/Visual Aids

Provide the children with real items that relate to the theme.

Talk About

Introduce the theme to the group with a simple picture book of the subject. Use the text of the book as the basis for the chant. Say a sentence and have the children echo it.

To Extend This Circle Time

Copy each phrase of the chant on large paper. Supply the children with washable markers, crayons or paint to illustrate the page. Bind the pages to create a big book about the theme and share it with the children. Place the book in the classroom library; the children will want to look at it again and again.

Head and Shoulders

Head and shoulders, knees and toes, knees and toes,
Head and shoulders, knees and toes, knees and toes,
Eyes and ears and mouth and nose,
Head and shoulders, knees and toes, knees and toes.

Body Awareness

Circle Time Starter

Invite the children to sit on the floor with their legs extended in front of them. As they sing the words to the song, ask them to stretch and touch each body part. Vary the actions by singing, stretching and touching while standing.

Props/Visual Aids

Designate an area in your classroom as your "measuring wall." Measure each child's height and mark it on the wall. Remeasure the children approximately every six weeks and record any changes on the wall. To show each child's growth, connect the measurements using a different color of yarn each time.

Talk About

Have the children line up from the smallest to the tallest. Measure the length of the children's feet, the distance between their knees and toes or the distance between their knees and shoulders. Graph the numbers on large chart paper. Ask, "What is longest distance? The shortest?"

To Extend This Circle Time

Choose a good exercise video for children. (You might try Disney's *Mousercise* or *Workout with Daddy and Me* from Family Home Entertainment. Check your public library for title availability.) Clear an adequate space in your large muscle area and encourage the children to exercise with you. Use a camcorder to create your own exercise video. Use this song for one of the segments and other Body Awareness Circle Times in this book for additional ideas.

Libby
Eric
Ben

Circle Time Starter

This song is a good basis for creating your own songs. The words can be lists of items, body parts, colors, letters of the alphabet or concepts relating to a specific theme.

Props/Visual Aids

Use a chart pad and markers to list the ideas to be included in the song. Simple drawings or pictures cut from magazines will give the children visual clues when reading the list. The ideas may be written before class, or ask the children to help you create the list.

Talk About

Create a web list of all the things the children know or that you want them to remember about the theme. If you were writing about bears, the web might include: hibernate; live in woods; brown, black or polar; eat grasses, fruits and fish; babies are called cubs. The song might be:

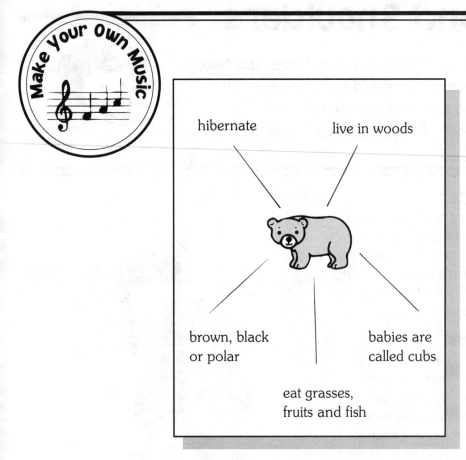

hibernate

live in woods

brown, black or polar

babies are called cubs

eat grasses, fruits and fish

"Brown and black live in the woods, in the woods,
Polar lives in the Arctic, the Arctic,
They eat fish and fruit and nuts,
Some will sleep all winter long, snore, snore."

To Extend This Circle Time

Add the song to the class songbook. Invite the children to add their illustrations of one or more of the concepts in the song.

Circle Time Starter

Vary the words to the song using different spatial concepts. You might sing,

"Up and down and in and out, in and out,
Up and down and in and out, in and out,
Turn around and around and around,
Up and down and in and out, in and out."

Props/Visual Aids

Provide large wooden blocks or low sturdy chairs. Use masking tape boundaries to create "areas" on the floor. The children can sit, step and move around these as they sing the song.

Talk About

Ask, "What are some other ways our bodies can move?" List the children's responses. Many of the actions they describe will have an opposite action. You might list "over and under," "run and stop," "hop on one foot and hop on the other foot." Sing the song again using the children's ideas.

To Extend This Circle Time

Divide the children into two groups. As you sing the song, have one group demonstrate one action and the other show the opposite action.

Tapes and CDs

Beall, Pamela Conn, and Susan Hagen Nipp. "Head, Shoulders, Knees, and Toes" from *Wee Sing Children's Songs and Fingerplays*. Price Stern Sloan, 1990.

Cassidy, Nancy. "Head, Shoulders, Knees, and Toes" from *Kids' Songs 2*. Klutz Press, 1986.

Raffi. "Tête, Epaules" from *Rise and Shine*. MCA Records, 1982.

I Know an Old Lady

*(A cumulative song: do not sing the words in parentheses
when the verses are sung in reverse order.)*

I know an old lady
who swallowed a fly.

I don't know why
she swallowed the fly.
Perhaps she'll die.

She swallowed a spider to catch the fly.
(It wriggled and wriggled and wriggled inside her.)

She swallowed a bird to catch the spider.
(How absurd to swallow a bird!)

She swallowed a cat to catch the bird.
(How about that! She swallowed a cat!)

She swallowed a dog to catch the cat.
(What a hog, to swallow a dog!)

She swallowed a cow to catch the dog.
(I don't know how she swallowed a cow.)

She swallowed a horse to catch the cow.
She died, of course!
*(You may prefer to choose a different ending:
"She showed no remorse" or
"She burped them all up!")*

Making Comparisons

Circle Time Starter
The animals the old lady swallows vary in size from very small to very large. As you sing the song, invite the children to use their hands and bodies to show how the animals get progressively larger.

Props/Visual Aids
Share your favorite picture book illustrations as you sing the song. (Check your library for Bernice Nadine Westcott's humorous version or Colin and Jacqui Hawkins' "lift-the-flap" book.) Or color, cut out and laminate the illustrations on page 44. Arrange the pictures in order to provide visual cues for the verses.

Talk About

Ask the children to remember a time when they ate a large amount of food. Ask, "How did your stomach feel then?" "How does it feel right before lunch?" Continue to make comparisons of how their bodies feel at different times: tired, awake, sick, well.

To Extend This Circle Time

Make a tray of fruit-flavored gelatin. Use animal-shaped cookie cutters to cut out the animals in the song. The children can eat the animals as they pretend to be the old lady.

Circle Time Starter

The old lady in the song ate a very strange meal. Sing the song again using the children's suggestions for real food. You might sing, "I know an old lady who swallowed some toast. She ate some toast, most of the toast." You can sing about breakfast, lunch, dinner or snack foods.

Props/Visual Aids

Use plastic models of food to use as prompts for the new verses you create.

Talk About

As the children choose foods for the song, talk about the category to which the food belongs. You can simplify the USDA's Food Pyramid's six basic food groups:

fats, oils and sweets	milk, yogurt and cheese
vegetables	meat, poultry, fish, beans, eggs and nuts
fruit	bread, rice, pasta and cereals

List these on chart paper or your chalkboard or use the simple drawings of representative foods on page 45. When selecting the foods for the old lady's "meal," be sure to choose foods from different food groups.

To Extend This Circle Time

Supply the children with playdough or clay to make their own models of food. After they have dried, paint the models with tempera paint. Use your dramatic play area to create a class restaurant. The children can make menus listing the foods they have made, and alternate in the roles of cooks, waiters and diners.

Tapes and CDs

Penner, Fred. "There Was an Old Lady" from *Ebeneezer Sneezer*. Oak Street Music, 1992.

Peter, Paul and Mary. "I Know an Old Lady Who Swallowed a Fly" from *Peter, Paul and Mommy, Too*. Warner Brothers, 1993.

Seeger, Peter. "I Know an Old Lady" from *Stories and Songs for Little Children*. High Windy Audio, 1989.

44

If You're Happy and You Know It

If you're happy and you know it, clap your hands,
If you're happy and you know it, clap your hands,
If you're happy and you know it,
Then your face will surely show it,
If you're happy and you know it, clap your hands.

Circle Time Starter

Vary the words to the song by using a different emotion for each verse. Have the children suggest actions to illustrate the emotions. They might include:

grumpy: you can growl   sad: you can cry
tired: you can yawn   hungry: rub your tummy
excited: jump up and down   scared: you can scream

Props/Visual Aids

Supply the children with paper plates and washable markers. Ask them to draw simple faces showing each emotion. As you sing the song, the children may hold up the plate illustrating the feeling or emotion for each verse.

Talk About

Discuss how people show their feelings. Ask, "How do you show that you are tired? Hungry? Sad? Angry?" Be sure to encourage discussion of appropriate and inappropriate ways to show feelings. Use the children's responses to create new actions for the song's verses.

To Extend This Circle Time

Supply the art center with large sheets of paper, glue, safety scissors and magazines. Ask the children to find pictures of people showing different expressions. Cut and glue to make a collage. You may want to make several collages, each one illustrating just one emotion. As the children search for pictures, help them sort the ones they choose into the selected categories. Label the finished collages and display them in the classroom.

Letter Recognition
Aa Bb Cc

Circle Time Starter

Vary the words to the song by choosing an initial consonant sound and a simple word that begins with that letter. You might sing,

> A book, book, book, starts with **B** . . .
> Take a look, look, look, at a book, book, book,
> Because a book, book, book, starts with **B**.
> or
> *Cat* starts with **C** . . .
> The cat, cat, cat chased a rat in a hat,
> And the cat, cat, cat, starts with **C**.

Invite the children to choose objects to sing about from items found around the room. As you choose rhyming words to complete the verses, remember to be silly!

Props/Visual Aids

Make life-sized paper bag puppets using grocery bags, one bag for each letter. Cut a hole in the top for the child's head. Cut out armholes on the sides of the bags. Supply the children with paint, glue, cut-out letters, stamps and stickers to decorate their letter "puppets." Make one set of large bags for your classroom or use small lunch bags and let each child make his or her own set.

Talk About

Choose a letter of the day. Ask the children to name items found in the classroom that begin with the letter. Place laminated signs and posters in easily accessible locations. Invite the children to circle the letter of the day with washable markers on the signs as they move throughout the room.

To Extend This Circle Time

Have a Letter of the Day party. Celebrate the letter by using playdough or clay to make models of the letter. Supply the art center with magazines, safety scissors and glue to make collages of things that start with the letter. Eat a snack that begins with the letter or make cut-out cookies in the shape of the letter.

Circle Time Starter
Vary the words to the song to make comparisons, focusing on size, shape, color, texture and so on. For a unit on recognizing colors, you might sing, "If you are wearing brown, please stand up" and "If you are wearing red, raise your hand."

Props/Visual Aids
Make flash cards showing the items you want to compare. You could use a simple sketch of the items or pictures cut from magazines on the cards.

Talk About
As you sing the new words to the song, hold up the flash card for each verse. Display the cards for the previous verses so that all are visible for comparison. Ask, "How are these two pictures different? How are these the same?" Invite the children to take turns choosing cards to sing about.

To Extend This Circle Time
Provide as many real items in the chosen category as possible. Involve parents in collecting items for the classroom. Allowing the children to touch and manipulate real items will help make their comparisons a more concrete experience.

Tapes and CDs

Beall, Pamela Conn, and Susan Hagen Nipp. "If You're Happy and You Know It" from *Wee Sing Children's Songs and Fingerplays*. Price Stern Sloan, 1990.

Greg and Steve. "If You're Happy and You Know It" from *We All Live Together*, *Vol. 3*. Youngheart Records, 1979.

Little Richard. "If You're Happy and You Know It" from *Shake It All About*. Disney, 1992.

Let Everyone Clap Hands Like Me

Let everyone clap hands like me (clap, clap)
It's easy as easy can be (clap, clap)
Let everyone join in the game (clap, clap)
You'll find that it's always the same. (clap, clap)

Body Awareness

Circle Time Starter
Vary the words to the song by choosing actions that focus on different body parts and movements. Some variations might include:

roll hands	tap toes	whistle
wink eyes	stamp feet	wave arms
shake heads	snap fingers	yawn

Props/Visual Aids
Display pictures of various body parts and ask the children to create actions for each part. Take photographs of the children performing the new actions to use as prompts when singing the song.

Talk About
Discuss the different movements and actions a part of the body can make. Ask, "How many ways can you move your head?" Make a group chart of the children's responses.

To Extend This Circle Time
Provide the children with large sheets of paper. In groups of two, have one child lie on the paper while the other traces around him or her with a crayon or washable marker. The children may then add details to their outlines. Display the finished drawings around the classroom.

Circle Time Starter
Vary the words to the song by using the names of the children in your group. Sing, "Let everyone clap hands like Jimmy." Jimmy may then begin the next verse by choosing an action and the name of a classmate.

Props/Visual Aids
Ask the children to bring photographs of themselves or take each child's picture at school. Hold each photo up as you sing the song together. When a child's picture is displayed, he or she may choose the action for the verse.

Talk About
This song is a great way for children to learn the names of their classmates. Create a chart of each child's favorite action and use the chart as you sing. Using the patterns on page 52, you can also make flash cards with the children's names and simple sketches depicting their favorite actions.

To Extend This Circle Time
Display pictures of the children participating in activities around the classroom. Write large or small group stories about the activities to share with parents. Provide the art table with paper, crayons or markers and mirrors. Encourage the children to draw self-portraits.

Circle Time Starter
Vary the words to the song by giving the children suggested movements around stationary items in the classroom. You might sing, "Let everyone sit on the chairs" or "Let everyone crawl under the table."

TLC10066 Copyright © Teaching & Learning Company, Carthage, IL 62321

Props/Visual Aids

Enlarge the pictures on pages 53 and 54 or draw simple illustrations to make picture cards for the song.

Talk About

Show a picture card to the children. Ask, "What words could we sing for this picture?" Sing the new verse and encourage the children to demonstrate the actions. You could also move the action outside where the children could move through the playground equipment following the song's directions.

To Extend This Circle Time

Use a camcorder to videotape the children as they sing the song and move around the playground or classroom. Invite the parents to view the video at an open house, or make it available for home viewing.

Tapes and CDs

McGrath, Bob. "Let Everyone Clap Hands Like Me" from *Sing Along with Bob, Vol. 2.* Kids' Records, 1985.

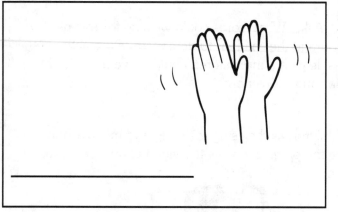

_____

_____

_____

_____

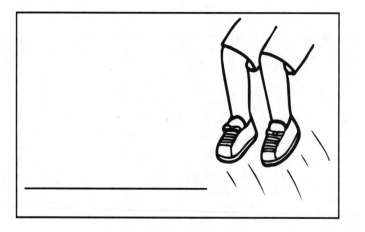

_____

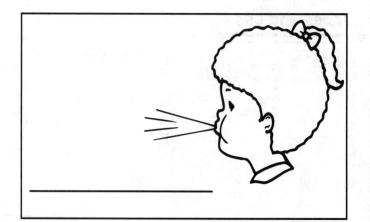

_____

52

The Muffin Man

Do you know the muffin man,
The muffin man, the muffin man,
Do you know the muffin man,
Who lives on Drury Lane?

Yes, I know the muffin man,
The muffin man, the muffin man,
Yes, I know the muffin man,
Who lives on Drury Lane.

Circle Time Starter

Vary the words to the song by using names and addresses or house colors of the children in the group. Sing, "Do you know Kayla B., Kayla B., Kayla B., do you know Kayla B., who lives on Maple Street?" or "Do you know Trevor C . . . who lives in a blue house?"

Props/Visual Aids

Using the pattern on page 59, have the children color a house to match their home. The drawings may be used as prompts when singing the song. Each child may hold up his or her picture as the class sings the verse about that child.

Talk About

Display a map of your community on the bulletin board. (Your local Chamber of Commerce is a good source.) Place a marker on your school's location and on the home of each child in the classroom. Don't forget to include your home! Group the children by neighborhood, distance or direction from the school. Ask, "Who lives the closest to school? Who lives the farthest?" Talk about routes to school and other local neighborhood destinations.

To Extend This Circle Time

Using the patterns on page 60, make a mobile for each child showing his or her birth date, address and phone number. You can also add learned skills, such as tying shoes, writing names or counting to 20. Begin by cutting a 9" (23 cm) paper plate into a spiral. Attach a piece of yarn to the center for hanging. Use yarn to add the cut-outs to the plate when a child masters a particular skill or concept. Display the mobiles in the classroom.

Circle Time Starter

Vary the words to the song by using workers and jobs in your community or neighborhood. Sing, "Do you know the firefighter . . . who lives at the fire station?"or "Do you know the grocer . . . who works at the food store?" or "Do you know the librarian . . . who works at the library?"

Props/Visual Aids

Bring in objects the person in the community might use for the job. Discuss how the firefighter's hat, the grocer's calculator and the librarian's book stamp help them in their work.

Talk About

Take the children on a field trip to a local business or invite parents to visit the class to talk about their jobs. Before each field trip or visit, ask the class to help you list the things they would like to know about that job. After the visit, create a web chart depicting "what we know about firefighters." Create and display group charts of different occupations.

To Extend This Circle Time

Arrange your dramatic play area to represent a fire station, bakery, grocery store or other community business. Try to provide as realistic props as possible. You may be able to borrow some items from a parent or business. Ask your class if they would like to start a class business. Possibilities might include a bake shop, car wash or greeting card store. Visit a similar business in your area and make lists of what you will need. Encourage lots of parent support, assign jobs and open for business. Who will your customers be? Other classes in school, teachers and staff, and of course, the parents!

Circle Time Starter

Ask a parent or other adult to visit the class as the "Muffin Man" (or "Muffin Mom"). The parent can dress in a chef's hat and apron with a dusting of flour on his or her face, and carry a mixing bowl and spoon. Plan a surprise entrance, while the children are singing the song.

Props/Visual Aids

Supply a variety of mixing bowls, spoons, muffin pans, whisks and other unbreakable utensils you might use in making muffins. As you sing the song, allow the children to take turns pretending to mix and bake muffins. Bring a variety of muffins for the children to taste. Create a bar graph to show the children's favorite kinds of muffins.

Talk About

A muffin can be part of a nutritious, simple breakfast. Discuss the importance of starting the day with a good breakfast. On chart paper, have the children help you make a menu of healthy breakfast foods.

To Extend This Circle Time

Make muffins with your class! You may choose one of the many muffin mixes available commercially or use the simple recipe below. Try adding bananas, nuts, blueberries, raisins, chopped and peeled apples or other fruit. If you make several varieties of muffins, you may wish to use mini muffin pans to allow the children to try several kinds in smaller quantities.

Sweet Best-Ever Muffins*

1³/₄ c. (420 ml) flour
½ c. (120 ml) sugar
2½ tsp. (12.5 ml) baking powder
³/₄ tsp. (3.75 ml) salt

1 beaten egg
³/₄ c. (180 ml) milk
¹/₃ c. (80 ml) cooking oil

Stir together flour, sugar, baking powder and salt; make a well in the center. Combine egg, milk and oil. Add all at once to dry ingredients and stir just until moistened. Fill paper cup lined or greased muffin pans ²/₃ full. Bake at 375°F (190°C) for 18 to 20 minutes. (Mini muffins will require less baking time.)
*Recipe from Better Homes and Gardens' Quick Breads Cookbook. Meredith Corporation, 1975.

Invite the children's parents to attend a breakfast of muffins, fruit and milk prepared and served by the class. Use page 61 for your invitations.

Tapes and CDs

Greenberg, Josh. "Do You Know the Muffin Man?" from *Rhythm and Rhymes*. A Gentle Wind, Inc., 1982.

Greg and Steve. "Muffin Man" from *We All Live Together, Vol. 2*. Youngheart Records, 1978.

Sharon, Lois and Bram. "Muffin Man" from *Singing 'n' Swinging*. Elephant Records, 1980.

We would like you to join us for breakfast!

Who: _____

What: _____

Where: _____

When: _____

Old MacDonald Had a Farm

Old MacDonald had a farm,
Ee-i-ee-i-oh.
And on this farm he had a (animal),
Ee-i-ee-i-oh.
With a (animal sound, animal sound) here,
And a (animal sound, animal sound) there,
Here a (animal sound)
There a (animal sound)
Everywhere a (animal sound, animal sound).
Old MacDonald had a farm,
Ee-i-ee-i-oh.

Circle Time Starter

Sing a few verses of the song with the familiar farm animals. Ask, "What if Old MacDonald had a zoo? A pet store?" "What if Old MacDonald lived in the woods? On a lake? In the desert?" Sing the song again using the children's responses.

Props/Visual Aids

There are many plastic animals of all types available. The children may want to bring several favorites from their own collections. Share these at group time and create new verses to the song. If possible, place the animals in your block area for dramatic play. Be sure to label the animals the children have brought from home.

Talk About

Ask, "What would Old MacDonald feed his animals?" "What do you think Mrs. MacDonald thought about all the animals?" "Which animals do you think were their favorites?" Use the children's responses to write a group story about the MacDonalds and their animals.

To Extend This Circle Time

Take a field trip to a farm, zoo or pet store. Before your trip, talk about the animals you will see. Have the children record their visit by drawing pictures of animals and collect these for a class book about the trip.

Community

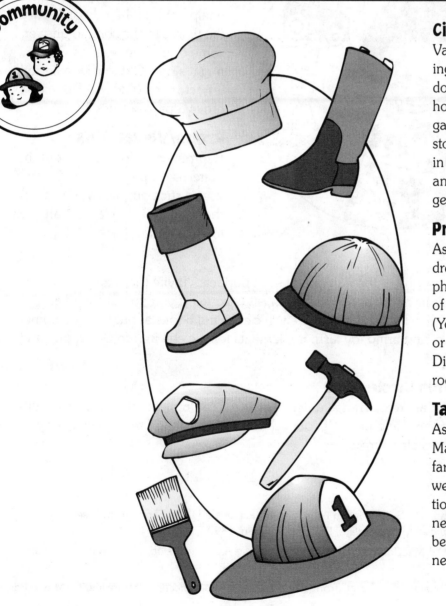

Circle Time Starter

Vary the words to the song by asking, "What might Old MacDonald do if he lived in your neighborhood? What would he have? A gas station? A bakery? A bookstore?" Talk about the businesses in the children's neighborhoods, and sing the song using their suggestions.

Props/Visual Aids

Ask a staff member or parent to dress as Old MacDonald and take photographs of him posing in front of some neighborhood businesses. (You may want to ask the owner's or manager's permission first.) Display these pictures in the classroom.

Talk About

Ask, "What clothes is Old MacDonald wearing to work on his farm?" "What would he need to wear if he had a bakery? A gas station?" "For which jobs would he need to wear a hat? Boots? A tool belt?" "What other things would he need to do his work?"

To Extend This Circle Time

Provide as many uniforms or work clothes as possible in your dramatic play area. Allow the children to choose articles of clothing and describe what jobs they can perform. Supply a variety of art materials such as paper towel tubes; small cardboard boxes and paper plates; along with glue, markers and paint. Encourage the children to construct the items they will need to perform their jobs.

Transportation

Circle Time Starter

How did Old MacDonald get around on his farm? How did he go to town? What types of farm equipment did he ride on? Vary the words to the song to answer some of these questions. You might sing, "Old MacDonald rode a tractor" or "Old MacDonald drove a pickup truck."

Props/Visual Aids

Reproduce, color and cut out the patterns on pages 65 to 67. To use as stick puppets as you sing the song, attach a large craft stick to each.

Talk About

Show the children one of the equipment stick puppets. Invite them to identify the vehicle and fill in its name as the group sings the song. If you do not live near a rural area, help the children identify the vehicles. Find books about farm equipment from your library and bring toy farm implements for the children to use in the dramatic play area.

To Extend This Circle Time

If you live in a rural area, arrange a field trip to a local implement dealer to see different types of farm equipment. If your school is in an urban area, check your yellow pages for possible sources.

Tapes and CDs

Beall, Pamela Conn, and Susan Hagen Nipp. "Old MacDonald Had a Farm" from *Wee Sing Children's Songs and Fingerplays*, Price Stern Sloan, 1990.

McGrath, Bob. "Old MacDonald Had a Farm" from *Sing Along with Bob, Vol. 2.* Kids' Records, 1985.

Raffi. "Old MacDonald Had a Band" from *The Singable Songs Collection.* Shoreline/A&M Records, 1988.

Various Performers. "Old MacDonald Had a Farm" from *Disney's Children's Favorites. Vol. 1.* Walt Disney Productions, 1979.

tractor

plow

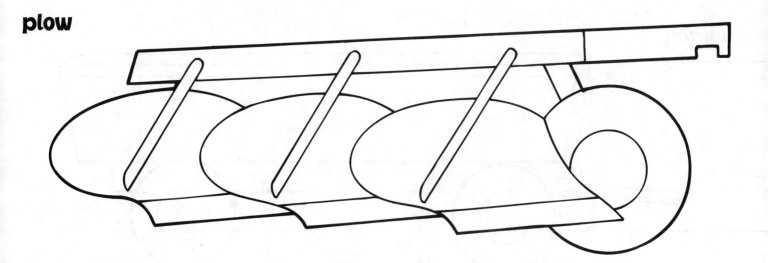

combine

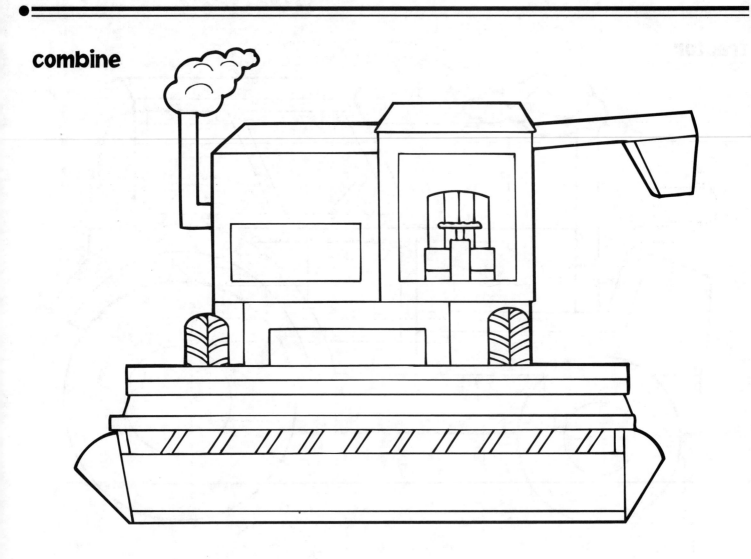

wagon

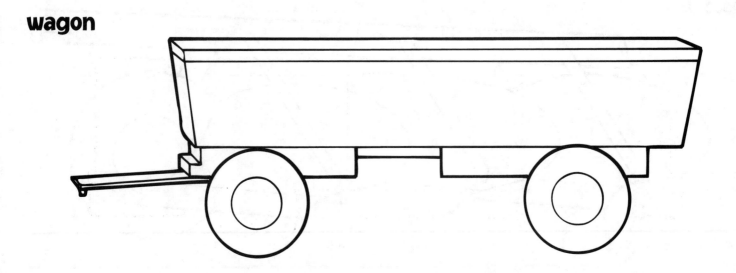

Put Your Finger in the Air

Put your finger in the air, in the air,
Put your finger in the air, in the air,
Put your finger in the air, and leave it there a year,
Put your finger in the air, in the air.

(additional verses)

Put your finger on your nose . . . and leave it till it grows
Put your finger on your head . . . is it green or red?
Put your finger on your chin . . . that's where the food goes in
Put your finger on your cheek . . . leave it there a week
Put your finger on your belly . . . shake it like it's jelly
Put your finger on your toe . . . put it just like so
Put your finger on your friend . . . now it is the end.

Body Awareness

Circle Time Starter

Sing the song together and have the children act out the words. Add your own verses, with the children's help. Choose a body part and write the word on a large sheet of paper. Ask for as many rhyming words as the children can think of and list them. Use these pairs of words to create new verses. Be sure to make the rhymes silly!

Props/Visual Aids

Use the pattern on page 71 to make a large hand with a pointing finger. Cut the hand out of sturdy tagboard and attach a large craft stick for a handle. (You could also use a large foam-rubber hand available at sporting events which fans wave to represent "We're number one!") Make sure each child has a turn to point to a body part with the big finger as you sing the verses.

68

To Extend This Circle Time

Ask the children what might happen if we had more or fewer of certain body parts. "What if you had four legs? What if you only had two teeth?" Supply the art center with large sheets of paper, crayons, washable markers or paint. Invite the children to paint pictures of themselves, imagining how they would look and what they could do with more or fewer of certain body parts.

Talk About

Help the children think of body parts from general to more specific. You may write the word *head* on a large sheet of paper. Ask, "What body parts are on or part of your head?" List the responses in a web which will include nose, ears, mouth, hair, eyes. Continue the list for each part (mouth might include tongue, teeth, lips) as the children generate ideas.

Circle Time Starter

Vary the words to the song to identify a letter of the alphabet. You might sing, "Put your finger on the *D* on the *D*."

Props/Visual Aids

Reproduce the alphabet on pages 72 to 77, one copy for each child. Make a large, similar alphabet on chart paper. You will also need sets of letters such as magnetic, foam or stencils.

Talk About

Give each child a copy of the alphabet pages. As you sing the song, invite the children to point to the letter you are specifying. Let the children take turns pointing to letters on the large chart paper. Sing the song as the children find the letters on their corresponding alphabet pages. Pass around the foam or plastic letter as you sing that letter's verse.

To Extend This Circle Time

Cut out a set of very large letters, 18" to 24" (46 to 61 cm) high, from newsprint. Invite the children to decorate or color the letters with washable markers, crayons, stickers, glue and colorful scrap paper. Display the letters around the room. As you sing the song again, have the children point to the large letters.

Circle Time Starter

Vary the words to the song to illustrate spatial concepts. You might sing, "Put your finger on the block," "Put your finger in the hole" or "Put your finger under the rug."

Props/Visual Aids

Have a variety of objects for the children to hold: blocks, empty paper rolls, spools. Invite the children to use them to demonstrate the words to the song.

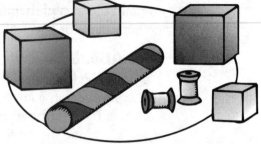

Talk About

As the children manipulate the objects, ask what they can or cannot do with a certain item. "Can you put your finger in the paper roll? Can you put your finger in the spool? Why not?"

To Extend This Circle Time

Set up an obstacle course in your large muscle area or gym. Use low tables, mats, climbers and other furniture for the children to climb over, under and through. Invite another class to visit your course.

Tapes and CDs

Glazer, Tom. "Put Your Finger in the Air" from *Children's Greatest Hits, Vol. 2*. CMS Records, Inc., 1977.

Greg and Steve. "Put Your Finger in the Air" from *Playing Favorites*. Youngheart Records, 1991.

Lehman, Peg. "Put Your Finger in the Air" from *Critters in the Choir*. Pal Music, 1989.

McGrath, Bob. "Put Your Finger in the Air" from *Sing Along with Bob, Vol. 2*. Kids' Records, 1985.

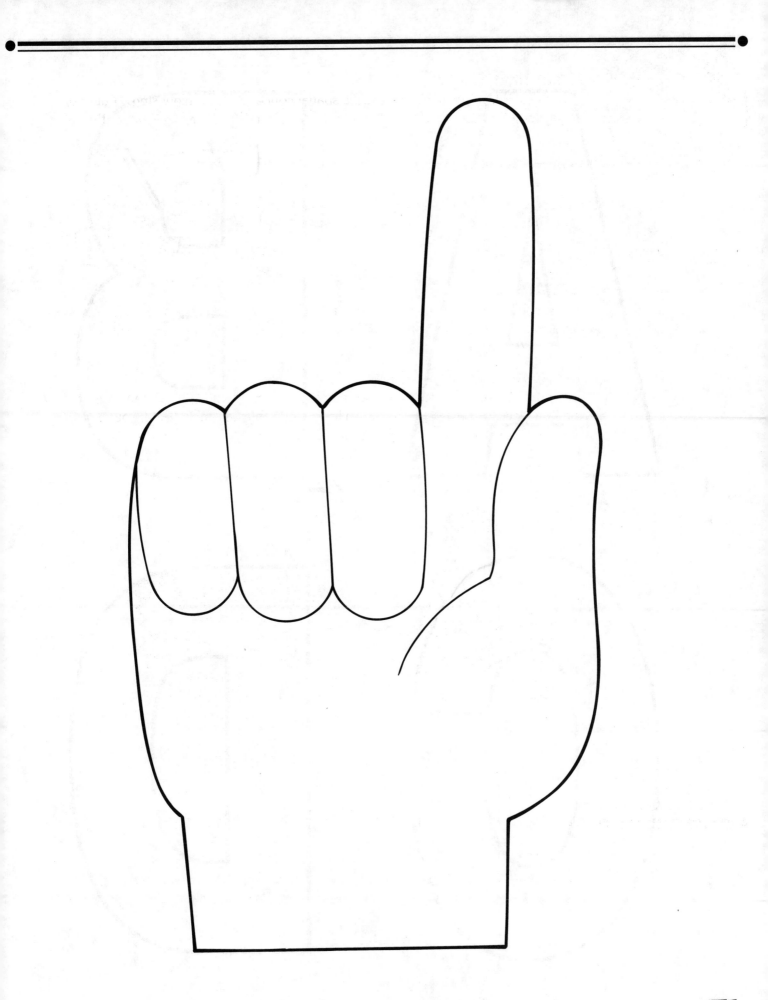

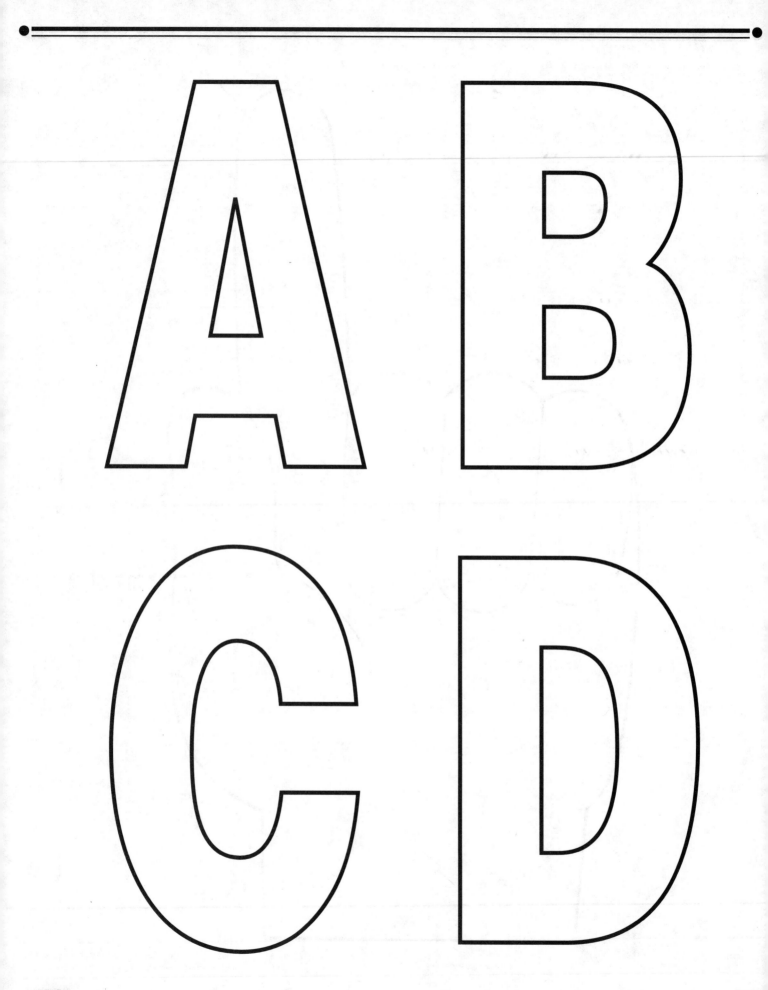

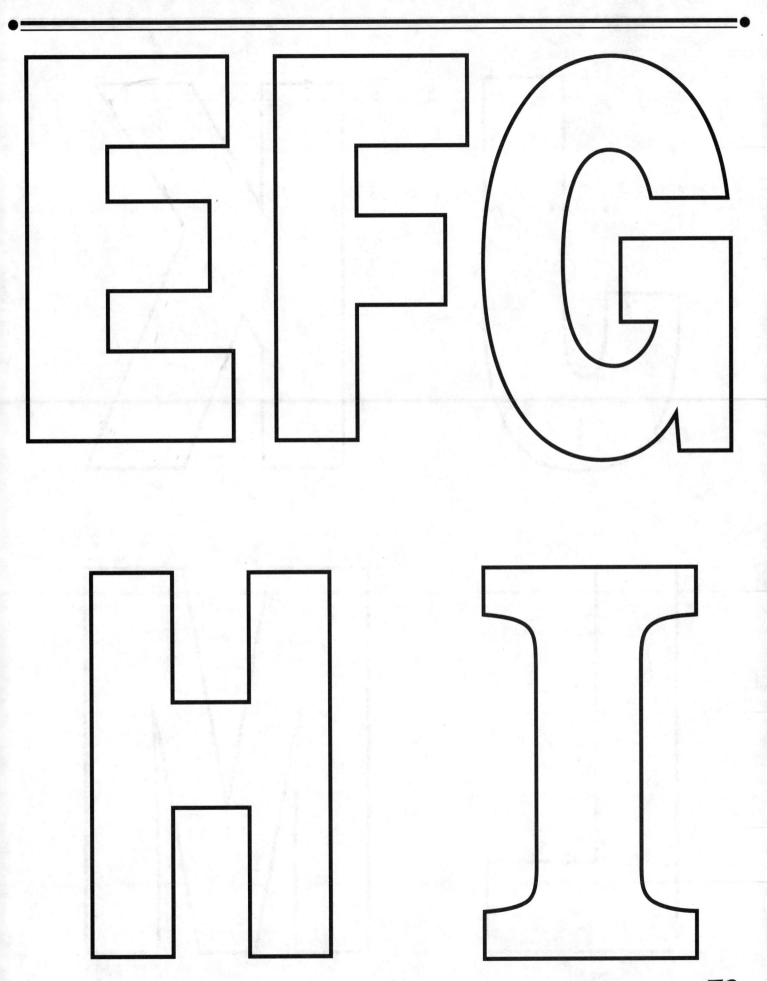

74

76

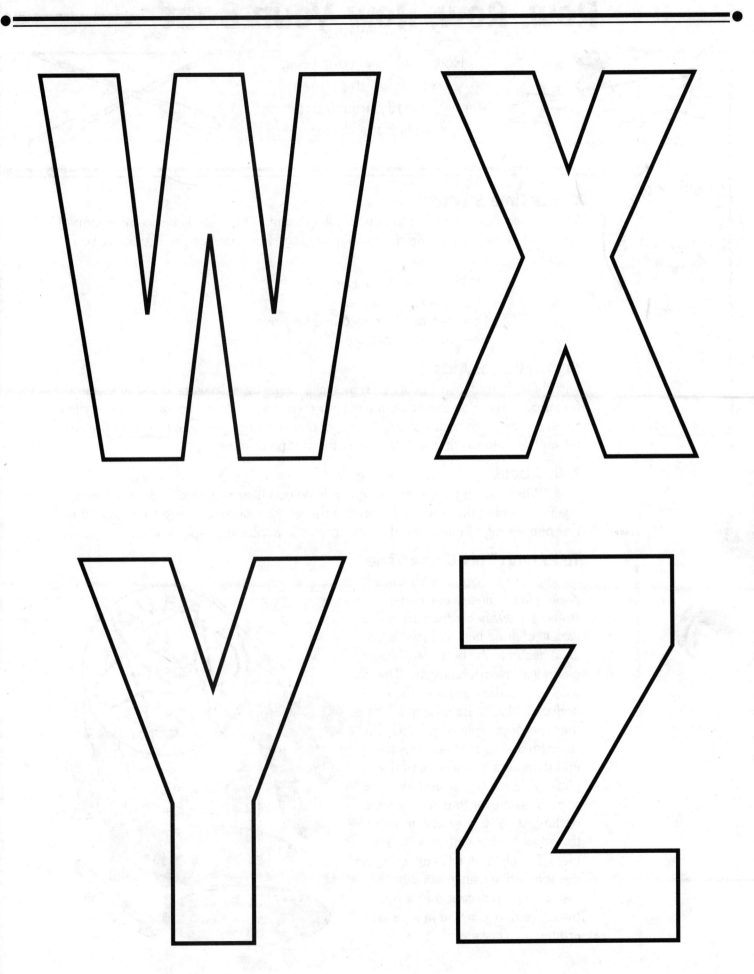

Row, Row, Row Your Boat

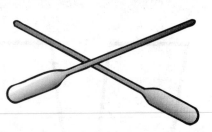

Row, row, row your boat,
Gently down the stream.
Merrily, merrily, merrily, merrily,
Life is but a dream.

Circle Time Starter

Vary the words of this song to fit your own theme. This melody invites repetition of key words, which the children will enjoy singing. For a unit on farm animals, you might sing,

> "Milk, milk, milk the cow,
> Milk her twice a day.
> Feed her, feed her, feed her, feed her,
> Feed her corn and hay."

Props/Visual Aids

Distribute rhythm instruments such as sticks, jingle bells, shakers, wood blocks and finger cymbals. You can easily make your own shakers by adding a few paper clips, small stones, dried beans or rice to empty film canisters. Be sure to secure the lids for enthusiastic shaking with several strips of tape or glue.

Talk About

Ask, "When we sing our song, what words do you hear repeated?" Sing the song again, accenting those words by singing them more loudly or more softly than the rest of the song. Finally, use the instruments to accent the repeated words.

To Extend This Circle Time

Supply your art center with small paper plates, glue, crepe paper streamers, washable markers and a variety of dried beans. Have each child decorate the bottoms of two plates with colorful designs. These will become the outside of the tambourine. Place a handful of beans in the bowl of one plate and circle the rim with a strip of glue. Attach several streamers to the edge of the plate. Add more glue and turn the second plate over to place it on top of the first. You may wish to secure the edges further with tape or staples. The children will enjoy singing the song while using their own instruments to accent the words. Invite them to join you in a parade around the classroom!

78

Nutrition

Circle Time Starter

Vary the words to the song to describe the vegetables you would use in a pot of soup. Ask, "What do you like in your soup?" You might sing,

"Shell, shell, shell the peas,
Put them in the pot.
Stir it, stir it, stir it, stir it,
I hope we make a lot!"

Other verses might include: "snap the beans," "scrub the carrots," "peel the onion" or "shuck the corn" and "eat it while it's hot!"

Props/Visual Aids

Bring in a variety of vegetables, some common and some more unusual. Leeks, zucchini, eggplant, mushrooms, turnips and bell peppers might be less familiar to the children than corn, potatoes, peas, beans and carrots.

Talk About

Encourage the children to examine the vegetables. Discuss how they are different and how they are the same. Ask, "Do you think this vegetable grows above the ground or below the ground?" "Do we eat the outside or the inside of this vegetable?" "Which vegetable is your favorite?"

To Extend This Circle Time

Make a pot of vegetable soup. Consider safety first in any cooking activity. Children can snap beans, shell peas and scrub carrots and potatoes. If you choose to allow the children to cut any vegetables, supervise the use of serrated safety knives found in many pumpkin carving kits. Children love to cook and will often try new and unusual foods if they have helped in the preparation. Invite other staff members, classes or parents to share the soup.

Transportation

Circle Time Starter

Sing this familiar song with your class. Ask, "What else can you do on a boat?" Use their ideas to create new first lines for the song. You might sing, "Toot, toot, toot the horn" or "Swish, swish, swish the waves" or "Drop, drop, drop the anchor."

Props/Visual Aids

Collect pictures of different types of boats. Invite the children to bring in their toy boats and ships. Be sure to label these prized possessions with the children's names. In your water table or a large dishpan, stage your own regatta with the boats.

Talk About

Discuss how the boats are alike and different. Ask, "Which boats need a sail and the wind to move?" "Which need a motor?" "What kind of boat might you use to go fishing?" Choose several categories to compare the boats and count how many you have of each type.

To Extend This Circle Time

Use a large cardboard box to create a boat for your dramatic play area. Have the children paint the outside and discuss possible names for your boat. Ask, "Where would you like our boat to take us?" Pack the boat with needed supplies and sail off on a wonderful journey!

Tapes and CDs

Beall, Pamela Conn, and Susan Hagen Nipp. "Row, Row, Row Your Boat" from *Wee Sing Sing-Alongs*, Price Stern Sloan, 1990.

McGrath, Bob, and Katharine Smithrim. "Row, Row, Row Your Boat" from *Song and Games for Toddlers*. Kids' Records, 1985.

Raffi. "Row, Row, Row" from *Raffi in Concert with the Rise and Shine Band*. Troubadour Records, 1989.

Various Performers. "Row, Row, Row Your Boat" from *Disney's Children's Favorites*, *Vol. 1*. Walt Disney Productions, 1979.

Skinnamarink

Skinnamarink a dink a dink
Skinnamarink a do
I love you.
(repeat)

I love you in the morning,
and in the afternoon,
I love you in the evening,
and underneath the moon.
(repeat chorus)

Circle Time Starter
Vary the words to the song by using the names of different family members. You might sing, "I love you, you're my mama, I love you, you're my dad, I love you, you're my sister, we're family and I'm glad."

Props/Visual Aids
Invite the children to bring photographs of family members or use the patterns on pages 84 and 85 to help the children make pictures of the people in their families. Each child can add these figures or photos to a poster showing all the people in his or her family. Ask each child to point to the pictures as you sing the song.

Talk About
Families are not all the same. Some families have one or two parents, some have grandmas or grandpas, aunts or uncles, or stepfamily members living in the home. Be sensitive to various family configurations and extended family patterns. Stress that "a family is the people who care about you!"

To Extend This Circle Time
In this mobile society, many children see their grandparents infrequently. Invite some grandparents from a nearby church or nursing home to be "adopted" by your class. Ask them to visit your classroom to share stories of when they were young or talents or skills such as woodworking, sewing or baking.

Feelings

Circle Time Starter

This is a great "buddy" song. Ask the children to stand close together in the circle and sing the song with a buddy. You may wish to teach the children simple motions for the chorus: *I* (point to self), *love* (cross arms over chest), *you* (point to buddy). Invite the children in for a group hug!

Props/Visual Aids

Use a large clock with movable hands to demonstrate the times of day mentioned in the song. You can make a clock from tagboard using a brass fastener to attach the hands; add the drawings (see patterns on page 83) to represent morning, afternoon, evening and the moon.

Talk About

Ask the children how they can show they care for friends, classmates, family members or people in the community. You can invite the class to participate in a community giving project. Children can bring items for a local food shelf or other charitable cause.

To Extend This Circle Time

You don't have to wait for Valentine's Day to have the class make cards telling special people that they care about them. Supply the art center with a variety of card-making materials, such as construction paper, washable markers, stamps and stickers. Have the children make cards to share with classmates, family or residents of a nearby nursing home.

Tapes and CDs

McGrath, Bob. "Skinnamarink" from *Sing Along with Bob, Vol. 1.* Kids' Records, 1984.

Sharon, Lois and Bram. "Skinnamarink" from *Sharon, Lois & Bram's Elephant Show Record.* Elephant Records/A&M Records, 1986.

Tia. "Skinamarink" from *Tia's Quacker Tunes.* Quacker T Productions, 1985.

Various Performers. "Skinnamarink" from *Car Songs: Songs to Sing Anywhere.* Kimbo, 1990.

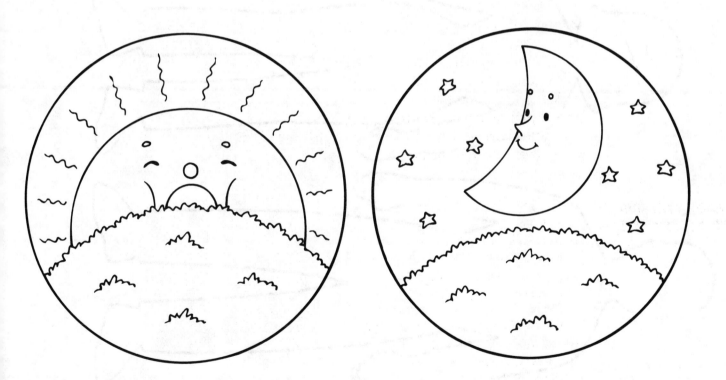

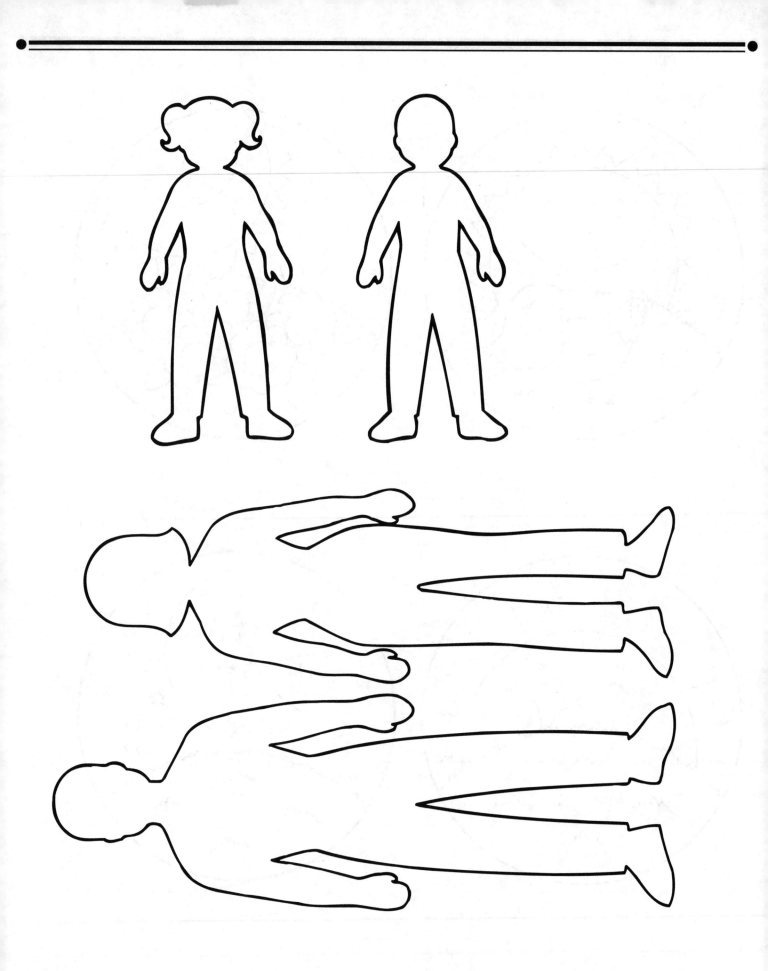

84

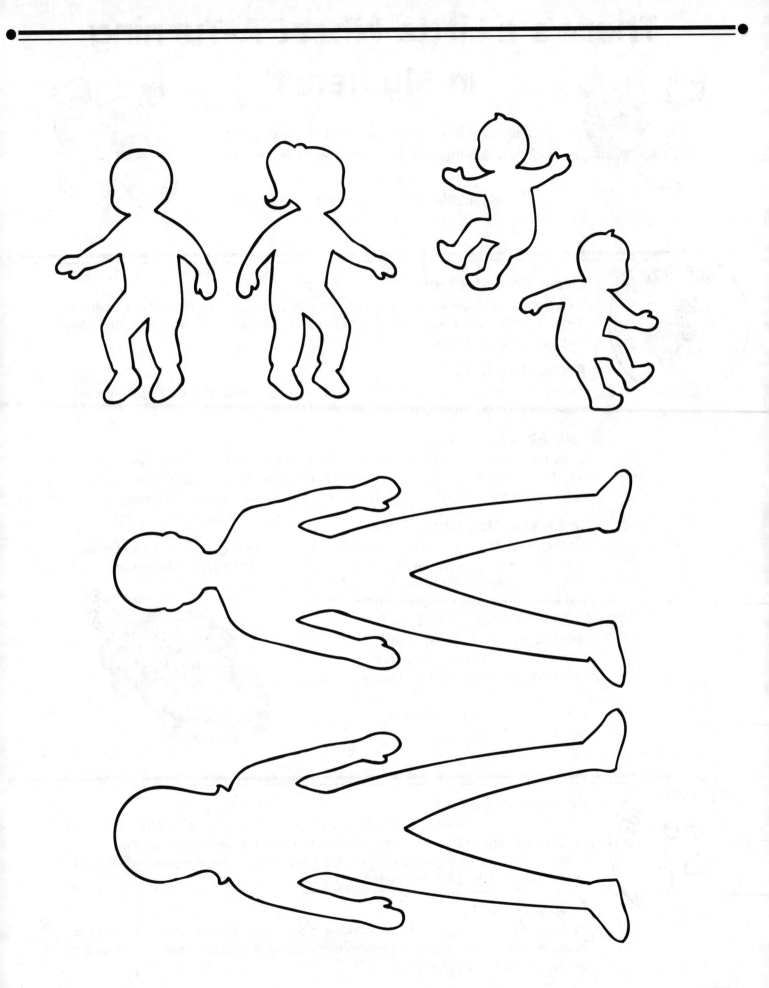

There's a Little Wheel A-Turning in My Heart

There's a little wheel a-turning in my heart,
There's a little wheel a-turning in my heart,
In my heart, in my heart,
There's a little wheel a-turning in my heart.

Feelings

Circle Time Starter
Vary the words to the song by singing about different feelings or emotions. You might sing, "There's a little wheel that's happy in my heart" or "There's a little wheel that's sleepy in my heart."

Props/Visual Aids
Enlarge and cut out the wheel patterns on page 88. Hold up the wheels to provide visual cues as you sing the new words to the song.

Talk About
Invite the children to share stories about times they were happy, silly, sleepy and so on. As they share their stories, give the children copies of the blank wheel patterns. Ask them to draw faces on their wheels to show the ways they were feeling.

To Extend This Circle Time
Use other parts of a car to expand on the children's feelings or emotions. On a large sheet of paper, draw a simple outline of a car. (Enlarge the pattern on page 89.) You might ask, "What makes you feel safe?" List their responses on the booster seat. "What makes you feel strong and powerful?" Write the answers on the engine. Other feelings and emotions might include: happy and bright–the headlights; tired–the tires; sad and crying–windshield wipers.

Letter Recognition Aa Bb Cc

Circle Time Starter
Vary the words to the song by choosing a letter to repeat throughout the verse as an initial consonant. You might sing, "There's a silly snake sleeping in my shoe" or "There's a big bat biking with a bear." Ask the children for suggestions when creating the verses. The sillier the better!

Props/Visual Aids
Make a large chart of items to be included in the verse. Ask the children to find or bring from home objects whose names begin with the selected letter. These may be displayed in a pocket chart.

86

Talk About

Write a group story using words that begin with the selected letter. You might use the verse from the song as your story starter. "The snake that sleeps in my shoe is named Sammy. He sips soda on Saturday and Sunday."

To Extend This Circle Time

Have the children illustrate their favorite silly verse. Use the pictures and stories to create a book, which the children can share with their families.

Circle Time Starter

Vary the words to this song by using parts of vehicles for each verse. Have the children help you create actions for the words. You might sing, "There's a little wheel a-turning on my car," "There's a little horn a-honking on my car" or "There's a little door a-opening on my car."

Props/Visual Aids

Visit a local auto dealership to pick up new car brochures. Cut out pictures of the automobile parts to use as prompts.

Talk About

Ask the children what types of cars their families have. How many have cars with two doors? Four doors? How many have mini vans? What colors are the cars? Create graphs to show the categories and the children's responses.

To Extend This Circle Time

Supply a variety of toy vehicles in your block area. Have the children help you make a roadway on the floor with masking tape. Take a field trip to a local auto dealer. Visit the repair garage and look at all the parts of cars. Ask a parent to bring in a small engine and explain how the different parts work together.

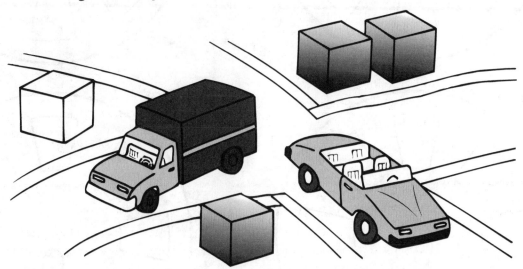

Tapes and CDs

Beall, Pamela Conn, and Susan Hagen Nipp. "There' a Little Wheel a Turnin'" from *Wee Sing Fun 'n' Folk*. Price Stern Sloan, 1989.

The Flyers. "Little Wheel a Turning" from *Your Smile*. Flyertunes Hootentoot, 1991.

Sharon, Lois and Bram. "There's a Little Wheel A-Turning in My Heart" from *Sharon, Lois & Bram's Elephant Show Record*. Elephant Records/A&M Records, 1986.

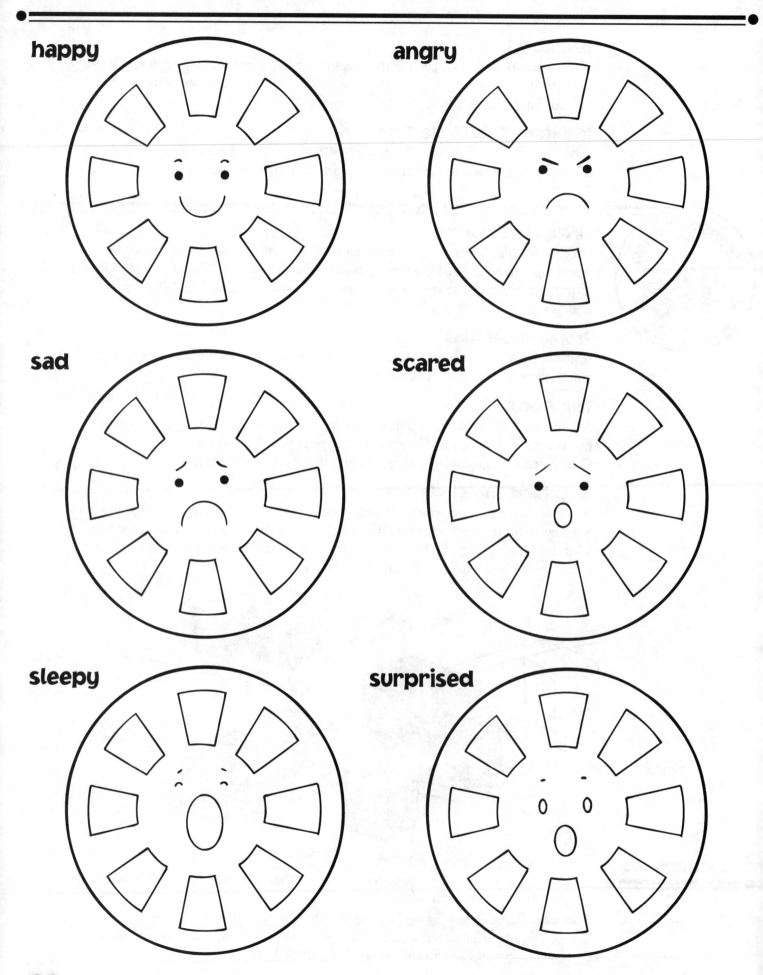

happy

angry

sad

scared

sleepy

surprised

The Wheels on the Bus

The wheels on the bus go round and round,
Round and round, round and round,
The wheels on the bus go round and round,
All through the town.

(additional verses)
The people on the bus go up and down . . .
The door on the bus goes open and shut . . .
The wipers on the bus go swish, swish, swish . . .

Classroom Friends

Hello, My Name is **Erin**

Circle Time Starter
Vary the words to the song using the names of the children in your group. Invite each child to choose a movement to go with his or her verse. You might sing, "Tammy's hands go clap, clap, clap"; "Cheng's feet go stamp, stamp, stamp" or "Marc's eyes go blink, blink, blink."

Props/Visual Aids
Take a photograph of each child in the class performing a different action. Use the pictures as prompts when singing the song.

Talk About
Young children may need lots of help when learning the names of their classmates. Singing songs using each child's name is a good way to help them in this process.

To Extend This Circle Time
Make a videotape of the children singing the song and performing the actions. Play the tape for the class. Invite the parents to a premier presentation of the video. Parents will enjoy seeing and learning the names of their children's friends. If some parents cannot visit the classroom, make the video available for overnight checkout.

Transportation

Circle Time Starter

As you sing the song, invite the children to think of actions to go with the verses. Create additional verses for the song. Ask, "What else happens on the bus?" Sing the song using a different type of transportation. Ask, "What could the words be if we sing about a bicycle? A tugboat? An airplane?" Write and then sing the verses using the children's suggestions.

Props/Visual Aids

Use chart paper when writing the additional verses for the song. Sketch a simple door, wheel, wiper, motor or whatever will serve as a reminder of which verse you are singing.

Talk About

Look at detailed pictures and talk about the parts of a variety of vehicles. Choose two vehicles and make lists of their similarities and differences. For example, following are partial lists comparing a boat and bicycle.

Same	Different
People ride on it	Boat has no wheels
Can pull things	Boat is in water, bicycle on road
Has a horn	How it is steered
Uses a light at night	Boat can have a motor

To Extend This Circle Time

Obtain several large cardboard boxes. Appliance stores are a good source. Cut windows, doors, hoods and trunks to make vehicles. You may wish to do this step when the children are not present. Then have the children paint the boxes. With a little creativity, they can make a boat, bus, semitrailer truck or train engine.

Tapes and CDs

McGrath, Bob. "Wheels on the Bus" from *Sing Along with Bob, Vol. 1*. Kids' Records, 1984.

Raffi. "Wheels on the Bus" from *Raffi in Concert with the Rise and Shine Band*. Troubadour Records, 1989.

Sharon, Lois and Bram. "The Wheels on the Bus" from *Sharon, Lois & Bram's Elephant Show Record*. Elephant Records/A&M Records, 1986.

Various Performers. "The Wheels on the Bus" from *Disney's Children's Favorites, Vol. 4*. Walt Disney Records, 1990.

Books to Share

Animals

Brown, Margaret Wise. *Big Red Barn.* Harper & Row, 1989. Rhymed text and illustrations introduce the many different animals that live in the big red barn.

Dunning, Michael. *Pets.* Macmillan, 1991. Introduces a variety of pets including dogs, cats, goldfish and hamsters.

Hoban, Tana. *A Children's Zoo.* Greenwillow Books, 1985. Color photographs of animals are accompanied by several descriptive words.

Ormerod, Jan. *When We Went to the Zoo.* Lothrop, Lee & Shepard Books, 1990. Touring the zoo, two children pet, ride and observe a variety of animals.

Royston, Angela. *Baby Animals.* Macmillan, 1992. Illustrations, photographs and text describe the appearance and behavior of such baby animals as a kitten, duckling and piglet.

Wellington, Monica. *The Sheep Follow.* Dutton Children's Books, 1992. After following various other animals they see going by, a herd of frolicking sheep is too tired to follow its shepherd.

Yabuuchi, Masayuki. *Whose Baby?* Philomel Books, 1985. Clear photographs introduce several animal infants and their parents.

Body Awareness

Cauley, Lorinda Bryan. *Clap Your Hands.* G.P. Putnam's Sons, 1992. Rhyming text invites the listener to roar like a lion, give a kiss, spin in a circle and perform other playful activities with the children and animals pictured.

Cummings, Phil. *Goodness Gracious!* Orchard Books, 1989. A child celebrates parts of her body while cavorting with a pirate, dog, cat, baboon and witch.

Dickens, Lucy. *Dancing Class.* Viking Penguin, 1992. Laura stretches, slides and dances in dance class.

Martin Jr., Bill, and John Archambault. *Here Are My Hands.* A celebration of human bodies points out various parts and their functions from "hands for catching and throwing" to "skin that bundles me in."

Offen, Hilda. *The Sheep Made a Leap.* Dutton Children's Books, 1994. As various animals perform in a show, the reader is encouraged to imitate their movements.

Classroom Friends

Hello, My Name is Erin

Anholt, Catherine. *All About You.* Viking, 1992. This book invites young children to think and talk about themselves and their world.

Cohen, Miriam. *Will I Have a Friend?* Aladdin Books, 1989. Jim's anxieties on his first day of school as he meets his classmates are happily forgotten when he finally makes a new friend.

Hennessy, B.G. *School Days.* Viking, 1990. Rhyming text and illustrations describe the familiar faces, routines and objects of a day at school.

Hoffman, Phyllis. *We Play.* Harper & Row, 1990. A simple, rhymed account of a child's fun-filled day at nursery school.

Community

Butterworth, Nick. *Busy People.* Candlewick Press, 1992. Simple questions and answers introduce 14 people who work around town, the things they do and the equipment they use, including a carpenter, doctor and grocer.

Isaacs, Gwynne. *While You Are Asleep.* Walker, 1991. While most people are asleep, others are pursuing their night jobs.

Mayer, Mercer. *Little Monster's Neighborhood.* Golden Press, 1978. A little monster describes people, activities and buildings in his town.

Miller, Margaret. *Guess Who?* Greenwillow Books, 1994. A child is asked who delivers the mail, gives haircuts, flies an airplane and does other important work.

Miller, Margaret. *Who Uses This?* Greenwillow Books, 1990. Brief text and photographs introduce a variety of objects, their purpose and who uses them.

Rockwell, Anne. *Come to Town.* Crowell, 1987. A visit to town includes stops at the school, the office, the supermarket and the library. Busy bears are everywhere!

Families

Carlson, Nancy L. *Louanne Pig in the Perfect Family.* Puffin Books, 1985. Louanne thinks she wants to be part of a big family until she spends a weekend with George and his five sisters and four brothers.

Gauch, Patricia Lee. *Christina Katerina and the Time She Quit the Family.* Putnam, 1987. When Christina quits her family so she can do whatever she pleases, ignoring her brother and her parents, she finds total self-reliance can sometimes be lonely.

Greenspun, Adele Aron. *Daddies.* Philomel Books, 1991. Simple text and black and white photographs depict some of the special things fathers do.

Hazen, Barbara Shook. *Why Couldn't I Be an Only Kid Like You?* Wigger Atheneum, 1975. Two young boys, one from a large family and the other an only child, wish they could exchange places.

Hennessy, B.G. *When You Were Just a Little Girl.* Viking, 1991. Grandma shares memories of treasured moments with her young listeners, memories that connect the generations.

Hoberman, Mary Ann. *Fathers, Mothers, Sisters, Brothers: A Collection of Family Poems.* Humorous poems celebrate every kind of family member, including aunts and uncles, stepbrothers and sisters, cousins and even cats!

Johnson, Angela. *One of Three.* Orchard Books, 1991. A series of candid reflections by the youngest of three sisters on her daily relationships with her older sisters and family.

Joosse, Barbara M. *Jam Day.* Harper & Row, 1987. An annual family reunion involving berry picking and jam-making reminds Ben that he is part of a big, noisy family of grandparents, cousins, uncles and aunts.

Scott, Ann Herbert. *On Mother's Lap.* McGraw-Hill, 1972. A small boy discovers that Mother's lap is a very special place with room for everyone.

Zolotow, Charlotte. *This Quiet Lady.* Greenwillow Books, 1992. In this simple celebration of the continuity of life, a child traces her mother's life through old pictures.

Feelings

Anholt, Catherine, and Laurence Anholt. *What Makes Me Happy?* Candlewick Press, 1994. Illustrated with detailed watercolors and in rhyming verse, children describe their feelings and what makes them feel that way.

Carlson, Nancy. *I Like Me!* Puffin Books, 1988. By admiring her finer points and showing that she can take care of herself and have fun even when there's no one else around, a charming pig proves the best friend you can have is yourself.

Conlin, Susan, and Susan Levine Friedman. *Let's Talk About Feelings: Nathan's Day at Preschool.* Parenting Press, Inc., 1991. Each page introduces a feeling Nathan had during everyday preschool situations. Questions encourage discussion to develop understanding.

Hubbard, Woodleigh. *C Is for Curious: An ABC of Feelings.* Chronicle Books, 1990. Bold design and humorous detail present an alphabet of emotions, from angry to zealous.

Kachenmeister, Cherryl. *On Monday When It Rained.* Houghton Mifflin Company, 1989. A young boy describes in simple, straightforward text and expressive photographs, the different emotions he feels each day.

Modesitt, Jeanne. *Sometimes I Feel Like a Mouse: A Book About Feelings.* Scholastic, Inc., 1992. A child imagines becoming a variety of animals while experiencing different feelings.

Bragg, Ruth Gembicki. *Alphabet Out Loud.* Picture Book Studio, 1991. Bold illustrations and poetic text depict a playful tour of the alphabet.

Carle, Eric. *All About Arthur (An Absolutely Absurd Ape).* Franklin Watts, Inc., 1974. To cure his loneliness, Arthur travels from city to city meeting other animals and also from A to Z.

Chouinard, Roger and Mariko. *The Amazing Animal Alphabet Book.* Doubleday & Company, Inc., 1988. Richly illustrated animals in alliterative phrases introduce the letters of the alphabet.

Duke, Kate. *The Guinea Pig ABC.* Dutton, 1983. Each letter of the alphabet is illustrated by a word which applies to the antics of some lively guinea pigs.

Ehlert, Lois. *Eating the Alphabet: Fruits and Vegetables from A to Z.* Harcourt Brace Jovanovich, 1989. A brightly illustrated alphabetical tour of the world of fruits and vegetables, from apricot and artichoke to yam and zucchini.

Martin Jr., Bill. *Chicka Chicka Boom Boom.* Simon & Schuster Books for Young Readers, 1989. An alphabet rhyme/chant that relates what happens when the whole alphabet tries to climb a coconut tree.

Bottner, Barbara. *Hurricane Music.* G.P. Putnam's Sons, 1995. Aunt Margaret's discovery of an old clarinet in the basement sets off a musical life-style for her and her family that includes jamming with hurricanes.

Catalana, Dominic. *Wolf Plays Alone.* Philomel Books, 1992. A wolf who wants to play his horn alone in the woods is joined by one noisy animal after another.

Griffith, Helen V. *Georgia Music.* Greenwillow Books, 1986. A little girl and her grandfather share two different kinds of music, that of his mouth organ and that of the birds and insects around his cabin.

Hawkins, Colin and Jacqui. *I Know an Old Lady Who Swallowed a Fly.* Putnam, 1987. A lively lift-the-flap book.

Kraus, Robert. *Musical Max.* Simon & Schuster Books for Young Readers, 1990. The peace and quiet following Max's decision to put his instruments away drives the neighbors just as crazy as his constant practicing did.

Stecher, Miriam B. *Max, the Music-Maker.* Lothrop, Lee & Shepard Books, 1980. Black and white photographs show Max finding music everywhere: in the roar of a train, in the purr of a pussy-cat and in the instruments he makes himself.

Butterworth, Nick. *Nice or Nasty: A Book of Opposites.* Little, Brown and Company, 1987. Funny, brightly colored illustrations of animals and humans introduce opposite concepts such as fast and slow, wet and dry, weak and strong.

Davis, Lee. *The Lifesize Animal Opposites Book.* Dorling Kindersley, 1994. Lively rhymes introduce life-size photographs of animal pairs, inviting comparisons.

Hoban, Tana. *Push • Pull, Empty • Full: A Book of Opposites.* Macmillan Publishing Company, 1972. Striking black and white photographs illustrate 15 pairs of opposites, such as front-back, first-last, push-pull.

My First Look at Opposites. Random House, 1990. Vivid, closeup photographs illustrate 15 pairs of opposites, such as big and little, up and down, full and empty, in and out and open and closed.

Spier, Peter. *Fast-Slow, High-Low: A Book of Opposites.* Doubleday & Company, Inc., 1972. Opposite concepts such as full-empty, strong-weak and more-less are illustrated by several pairs of contrasting pictures.

Westcott, Nadine B. *I Know an Old Lady Who Swallowed a Fly.* Little Brown, 1980. A humorous version of this favorite song.

Nutrition

Caseley, Judith. *Grandpa's Garden Lunch.* Greenwillow Books, 1990. After helping Grandpa in the garden, Sarah and her grandparents enjoy a lunch made from home-grown vegetables.

Ehlert, Lois. *Growing Vegetable Soup.* Harcourt Brace Jovanovich, 1987. In bright pictures, a child and father plant and grow vegetables and cook them to make the best soup ever.

Leedy, Loreen. *The Edible Pyramid: Good Eating Every Day.* Holiday House, 1994. Animals visit The Edible Pyramid, a restaurant that serves all kinds of delicious and nutritious meals.

Roffey, Maureen. *Mealtime.* Four Winds Press, 1983. Simple questions and bright, detailed art encourage children to talk and learn about mealtimes.

Root, Phyllis. *Soup for Supper.* Harper & Row, 1986. A new folktale about a wee small woman who catches a giant taking vegetables from her garden. She finds they can share both vegetable soup and friendship.

Suhr, Mandy. *When I Eat.* Carolrhoda Books, 1992. Bright illustrations and simple text explain how people, animals and plants eat and make use of their food.

Spatial Concepts

Asch, Frank. *Baby in the Box.* Holiday House, 1989. Baby, a fox and an ox play with blocks in and out of a box.

Gibbons, Gail. *Playgrounds.* Holiday House, 1985. Cheerful illustrations introduce swings, slides, merry-go-rounds, sandboxes, jungle gyms and other things to crawl through, climb on and run around at the playground.

James, Betsy. *Natalie Underneath.* Dutton Children's Books, 1990. Natalie and her brother Thomas enjoy being underneath various things as they play enthusiastically with their patient father.

Transportation

Brown, Craig. *Tractor.* Greenwillow Books, 1995. A farmer uses his tractor to tow the plow, disc, planter, cultivator, picker and other machines that help him grow a healthy crop of corn to sell at a roadside stand.

Coulter, Hope Norman. *Uncle Chuck's Truck.* Bradbury Press, 1993. Uncle Chuck's truck bounces over bumps and slides in the mud, all around the farm as he and his nephew do chores.

Florian, Douglas. *An Auto Mechanic.* Greenwillow Books, 1991. Simple text and colorful illustrations describe an auto mechanic working with cars, checking the engine and brakes, changing the oil and filters, fixing anything that is wrong.

Gibbons, Gail. *Emergency!* Holiday House, 1994. When there is an emergency, police, ambulance personnel, firefighters, pilots and the Coast Guard spring into action with their specialized equipment.

Levinson, Riki. *I Go with My Family to Grandma's.* E.P. Dutton, 1986. As five cousins and their families arrive by various means of transportation, Grandma's house in Brooklyn gets more and more lively.

Newton, Laura P. *William the Vehicle King.* Bradbury Press, 1987. William gets caught up in play with his racing cars, sedans, vans, trucks, steamrollers and other motor vehicles. He turns his bedroom rug into a super vehicle-filled highway.

My First Look at Things That Go. Random House, 1991. Simple text and clear photographs depict various forms of transportation, such as boats, trucks, planes and spaceships.

Royston, Angela. S*hips and Boats.* Macmillan, 1992. Text, illustrations and photographs introduce such ships and boats as the tugboat, paddle steamer, power boat and container ship.